Paula Nadelstern's
KALEIDOSCOPE QUILTS

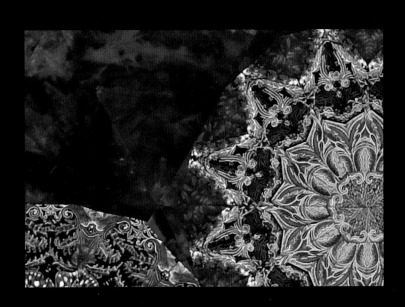

An Artist's Journey Continues

C&T PUBLISHING

Text copyright © 2008 by Paula Nadelstern

Artwork copyright © 2008 by Paula Nadelstern and C&T Publishing, Inc.

Publisher: Amy Marson

Creative Director: Gailen Runge

Acquisitions Editor: Jan Grigsby

Editors: Candie Frankel and Kesel Wilson

Technical Editors: Helen Frost and Joyce Lytle

Copyeditor: Alix North

Proofreader: Wordfirm Inc.

Cover Designer/Book Designer: Kristen Yenche

Production Coordinators: Zinnia Heinzmann and Casey Dukes

Illustrator: Kirstie Pettersen

Photography by Luke Mulks and Diane Pedersen of C&T Publishing unless otherwise noted

Published by C&T Publishing, Inc., P.O. Box 1456, Lafayette, CA 94549

The full quilt photos on the following pages were photographed by Karen Bell: 11, 18, 20, 29, 34, 37, 40, 43, 46, 51, 59, 73 and 124.

Kaleidoscope interior images: on page 2 Paul Knox Studios; pages 68, 70, 79, 90, 110 Charles Karadimos; page 91 Al Teich; page 94 Randy and Shelley Knapp of Knapp Studios; page 115 Peggy and Steve Kittelson.

Library of Congress Cataloging-in-Publication Data

Nadelstern, Paula.

Paula Nadelstern's kaleidoscope quilts : an artist's journey continues / Paula Nadelstern.

p. cm.

Includes index.

Summary: "Book features 19 Nadelstern Kaleidoscope quilts, 18 of which have not been previously published. Author also includes comprehensive technique and design chapters detailing her unique style and philosophy."--Provided by publisher.

ISBN 978-1-57120-503-2 (paper trade : alk. paper)

1. Quilting--Patterns. 2. Patchwork--Patterns. 3. Kaleidoscopes in art. I. Title.

TT835.N3275 2008

746.46'041--dc22

2008002009

Printed in China

10 9 8 7 6 5 4 3 2 1

To my best friends, Eric and Ariel.

Thanks for sharing your journeys with me and for coming along on mine.

CONTENTS

FOREWORD   4

INTRODUCTION   4

QUILT GALLERY   5

   KALEIDOSCOPIC XV: Eccentric Circles   7

   KALEIDOSCOPIC XVI: More Is More   11

   KALEIDOSCOPIC XVII: Caribbean Blues   15

   KALEIDOSCOPIC XVIII: Chai   18

   KALEIDOSCOPIC XIX: Tulips in the Courtyard Below   20

   KALEIDOSCOPIC XX: Elegant After Maths   23

   KALEIDOSCOPIC XXI: The Thank Your
      Lucky Star Memorial Quilt   26

   KALEIDOSCOPIC XXII: Ice Crystals   29

   KALEIDOSCOPIC XXIII: Cathy's Quilt   32

   KALEIDOSCOPIC XXIV: Ebb & Flow   34

   KALEIDOSCOPIC XXV: It's About Time   37

   KALEIDOSCOPIC XXVI: Big Red Chorus Line   40

   KALEIDOSCOPIC XXVII: September 11, 2002   43

   KALEIDOSCOPIC XXVIII: The Great Round-Up   46

   KALEIDOSCOPIC XXIX: How to Piece a Spiral   48

   KALEIDOSCOPIC XXX: Tree Grate, 53rd and 7th   51

   KALEIDOSCOPIC XXXI: The Other Side of the Circle   55

   KALEIDOSCOPIC XXXII: My Brooklyn Bridge   59

   KALEIDOSCOPIC XXXIII: Shards   63

THE ARTFUL KALEIDOSCOPE   66

   My Piece Policy   68

   My Design Strategies   70

   My Fabric   79

THE TECHNICAL KALEIDOSCOPE   88

   My Tools   90

   How to Draft an Angle   91

   Templating   94

   Power Piecing   110

   Finishing   115

WORKBOOK   118

   Kaleidoscope A   118

   Kaleidoscope B   120

APPENDIX   122

ABOUT THE AUTHOR   123

ACKNOWLEDGMENTS   124

SOURCES   125

INDEX   126

# FOREWORD

MASTER OF SYMMETRY: THE ART OF PAULA NADELSTERN

Every artist must find a voice that feels true and strong. Paula Nadelstern found hers early in her career as a quilt artist, inspired by a bolt of sensuous and beautiful Liberty of London fabric. The bilateral symmetry of the design was an epiphany that stirred Nadelstern's imagination and that has yielded a seemingly infinite vein of creative expression for more than twenty-five years.

Focusing first on the kaleidoscopic quality in the symmetry, Nadelstern innovated new techniques and developed a highly refined, intricate, and distinctive personal aesthetic. The incorporation of related crystalline forms, notably snowflakes, has continued to lead Nadelstern through an artistic evolution that has encompassed science, history, innovation, and tradition. Each composition offers a fresh revelation of the complexities inherent in Nadelstern's labor-intensive approach. Minute pieces of fabric are joined like slivers of colored glass into a magical whole, the masterful manipulations of color and pattern resulting in scintillating wheels, shifting ellipses, and other movements across the surfaces of the textiles.

Employing a technique that is counterintuitive to the conventional quilt process, Nadelstern obscures the seams that join pieces of fabric. The effect is a fluid rather than static surface, untethered by restraining grids. In the truest tradition of American quiltmaking, Nadelstern generously shares her imagination, techniques, and talent through workshops and publications and has been widely recognized and celebrated for her achievements. The hard-edged, fractal structure of snowflake and kaleidoscopic images might seem inimical to the seductive softness of a quilt, but in Paula Nadelstern's unique quilt idiom, this provocative tension erases the historical divide between art and quilt.

Stacy C. Hollander, Senior Curator of the American Folk Art Museum, New York

# INTRODUCTION

I've been told that I write books pretty much the same way that I make quilts. Fabric by fabric. Choice by choice. In a word, slowly. Although my everyday life often rushes past the particulars, my creative life celebrates them. I've found essential words, words I can live by, embedded in my quilting: *insight, imagination, nuance, mastery, grace*. For me, art is in the details.

I make my quilts on the same block in the Bronx where I grew up. We are three generations living within a block of each other on this most northern New York City street: my daughter, my mother, my mother-in-law, my husband, and me. For over twenty-five years, my workspace in our ninth floor, two-bedroom, cram-packed-with-fabric-and-sewing-stuff apartment was the 42-inch round kitchen table. Our perpetual dining companion was a Singer Featherweight, purchased for $25 at a yard sale. I used to call it an old machine until I learned it was a year younger than I am. Together we made my first quilt (a comforter cover, really) in 1968 in my college dorm. We continued as a team through the first twenty-seven quilts in my kaleidoscopic series. Today, I work in a 15-by-10-foot studio revamped from my daughter's former bedroom. Picture ceiling-high cupboards stuffed with fabric, drawers overflowing with the paraphernalia quilters collect, 6 feet of design wall, and a Bernina poised for action on a 4-by-6-foot counter.

My interest in things kaleidoscopic began in 1987 when I was struck by a bolt of fabric—a sumptuous, sinfully expensive, bilaterally symmetrical Liberty of London cotton known as Tana Lawn. Little did I know that purchasing a quarter yard would change my life forever, leading me, three years and four quilts later, to the state-of-the-art kaleidoscope and a new career. The insight from this anecdote is obvious: buy that piece of fabric no matter how expensive it is. As I peer through the incredible kaleidoscopes I have garnered over the years, like a sleuth searching for clues, I discover my design inspiration all over again. Who knows what the next turn of the scope will reveal, to me or to you?

Paula Lyman Nadelstern
September 2008

QUILT GALLERY

KALEIDOSCOPIC XV:
ECCENTRIC CIRCLES

1995, Bronx, NY

59″ × 75½″

Textiles: Cottons, silk, painted cotton by Skydyes

Techniques: Machine pieced, hand quilted

To me, my quilts are more about spatial relationships than math, which I'm not very good at. What I know to be true is that when joined together, the wedges, no matter how many there are, must equal 360°, the same number of degrees as there are in a circle.

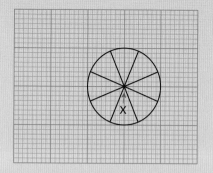

Did I figure out how to push the scope off-center because I understood the geometry? I don't know. What I do know is that it took fifteen quilts before this relationship made sense and when it did, it felt intuitive. On graph paper, I used a compass to draft a 16″ circle and then dissected it into eight 45° wedges. I moved the compass point (Y) a few inches to the left of the first circle's midpoint (X), opened it up so it was as wide as the distance to the original circle's circumference, and drew a second circle. The new circle matches the base of Triangle A, getting wider as it encircles the original until it extends to its full size in Triangle E. I extended the lines of the triangles into the new circle. This arrangement calls for one single Triangle A and Triangle E, but B, C, and D each need both a left and a right version.

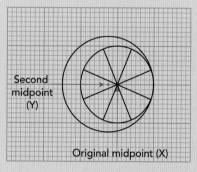

Second midpoint (Y)

Original midpoint (X)

Sometimes a quilt is creative kindling for another or a response to the last. What if, rather than distinguishing the second circle as a crescent shape with a highly contrasting fabric, the outlines between the first and second circles are ignored, filling the triangles as they get consecutively bigger with a continuation of the kaleidoscopic patterns? This "what if" question became the creative springboard for my next quilt.

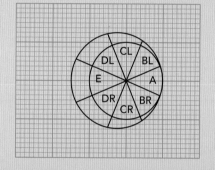

In the body of the quilt, I ran the nap of a French tapestry-like silk, purchased in the NYC garment district, in one direction. In the fractured border, I cut it randomly so light bounces off the surface erratically.

Hand-quilted concentric circles set up a textured rhythm that echoes the theme of the quilt. The circular quilting pattern radiates from the midpoint of the larger circle that encompasses the crescent shape.

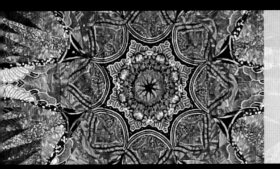

Portions of the stunning kaleidoscopic carpet covering the skywalks, ballrooms, prefunction areas, and elevator lobbies in the Hilton Americas-Houston hotel, connected to the George R. Brown Convention Center in Houston, Texas, were inspired by designs in this quilt and others made before 1995.

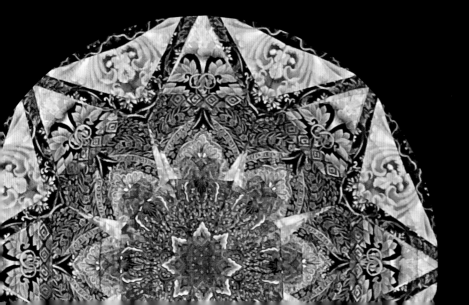

KALEIDOSCOPIC XVI:
MORE IS MORE

1996, Bronx, NY

64˝ × 64˝

Textiles: Cottons, silk

Techniques: Machine pieced, hand quilted

Many kaleidoscope makers have a preference for a thinner wedge, considering a complex effect more sophisticated and apt to sustain an adult's attention longer. Sixteen, seventeen, twenty-four triangles are possible. As attracted as I am to the intricacy offered by more, the angle of my wedges is restrained by my medium: how many points of fabric, surrounded by seam allowance, fit neatly into the center? For me, the maximum answer is ten.

But, what if I make twelve identical 30° wedges, sew them together into pairs, whack a few inches off each combined peak, and replace the missing portion with one 60° patch? By camouflaging the seam, the eye does not see that the center is a tidy six wedges, each bifurcating into two. The impression is of fast-moving abundance throbbing with activity.

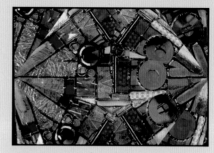

Kaleidoscope interior by Sea Parrot Kaleidoscopes.

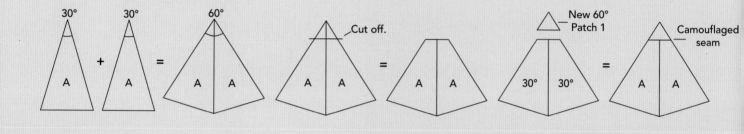

The twenty-nine small scopes bordering the quilt were inspired by the mirror configuration of a kaleidoscope by Sea Parrot Kaleidoscopes of Kennebunkport, Maine. This time, instead of making twelve identical wedges, I made six A wedges and 6 B wedges, sewed an A and a B together, and gave them a common gray-colored top. I used this same fabric to add thin strips of leading. The scopes are patches of cotton and silk to simulate the glow of dichroic glass incorporated in the object cases. Dichroic glass is coated with thin layers of titanium and zirconium, which allow some wavelengths of light to pass through but deflect others. This causes the glass to change color depending on the angle of light falling upon it.

Functioning as six-sided hexagons, these blocks were arranged like a traditional pyramid quilt, which I worked out on a graph paper grid, putting background fabric in the empty triangles. On graph paper, the composition is straightforward: four rectangles framed by a wide border.

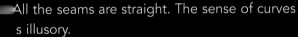

All the seams are straight. The sense of curves is illusory.

The most difficult task was creating what appears to be one continuous background, giving the impression the scopes sit on an uninterrupted, seam-free whole cloth. This effect meant using the same background to visually blend with itself. The ground is composed of two different cottons. Only in the quilt's extreme center is it placed randomly.

Kaleidoscopic XVI: More Is More was voted among the "100 Best American Quilts of the 20th Century" by a national panel of quilt experts in 1999.

KALEIDOSCOPIC XVII :
CARIBBEAN BLUES

1997, Bronx, NY

66″ × 71″

Textiles: Cottons, cotton blends, silk

Techniques: Machine pieced, hand quilted

hat did I know when I started this quilt? I knew I wanted to continue the technique conceived during the previous quilt: combine two thin wedges into a single triangle topped with a common Patch 1. This time I opted for two 22½° wedges merging into a 45° triangle. I knew I wanted to push the mandalas away from center stage and off the quilt's edge for the first time. I knew I would be traveling a lot during its construction with more downtime away from home than at home. If I could make a couple of what-to-do-next decisions at home, I'd know exactly which fabrics to schlep along, in case there were chances to sew on the road.

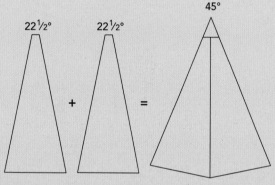

I was intrigued with conveying a sense of randomness in the background, partly as a reaction to the fussy background of the previous quilt, and partly to suggest the gorgeous shimmer of the sea. But piecing randomness turns out to be a lot more time-consuming than following a formula. (Instead, I made sixty-four 24″-long identical wedges, with the potential to build four 48″-wide mandalas with sixteen triangles each. The first sixteen inches would become the mandala. The last eight inches were designated background, using only fabrics from a water-colored palette mixed of silks and cotton.)

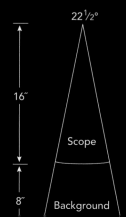

The final composition didn't slice off any of the mandalas' scalloped edges, but I was ruthless with the background blues and turquoises, rotary cutting them at differing amounts so when patched together, they bashed against themselves haphazardly. Leftover background formed the border.

One of my proudest achievements was figuring out how to animate the mandalas. All I had to do to set them in motion was to sew badly! See how the golden-yellow darts are all different sizes? Remember, all of the finished wedges are identical to each other. But in sewing the pairs together, when the needle arrived at this fabric sometimes I maintained the $1/4''$ seamline, sometimes I swerved and made a narrower seam (for a wider patch), and sometimes I did the opposite (fat seam, skinny patch). This imperfection renders a sparkling effect, especially combined with the sparkly irregular center.

KALEIDOSCOPIC XVIII:
CHAI

1998, Bronx, NY

37″ × 37″

Textiles: Cottons, silks

Techniques: Machine pieced, hand quilted

The second group exhibition by members of the Manhattan Quilters Guild, an eclectic group of professional fiber artists who meet in New York City, was titled *Yardworks*. The rules were relatively simple: construct a quilted work within the constraint of one square yard, both literally and metaphorically.

Figuring a yard is where one plays, I rationalized my way toward an asymmetrical sixteen-point image based on the interior of DELTA II, a limited edition kaleidoscope by Charles Karadimos of Damascas, Maryland.

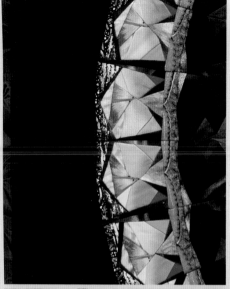

Rendering a spiral meant that none of the wedges were the same patchwork arrangement, although they were all the same angle. I drew half the kaleidoscope to scale, then followed the detailed map to make corresponding templates. Actually, every template for every patch was used only twice, once facing right side up, and then flipped over to be used a second time in a mirror image. The background is patched together from many textured black silks, each stabilized with a fusible woven interfacing.

The crucial Hebrew word *chai* refers to life. Used as a symbol, the word expresses the hope and prayer for life, health, and prosperity. In Hebrew, each letter represents a number (as if A equals 1 and B equals 2). The word *chai* is spelled *chet* (the 8th letter) plus *yud* (the 10th letter), making the numerical equivalent of *chai* eighteen. Consequently, the number 18 is also a symbol of life. This quilt is the eighteenth in my series.

In the end, the quilt measured 37 inches square and, rather than slice off the important black edge that causes the image to float, I started another quilt.

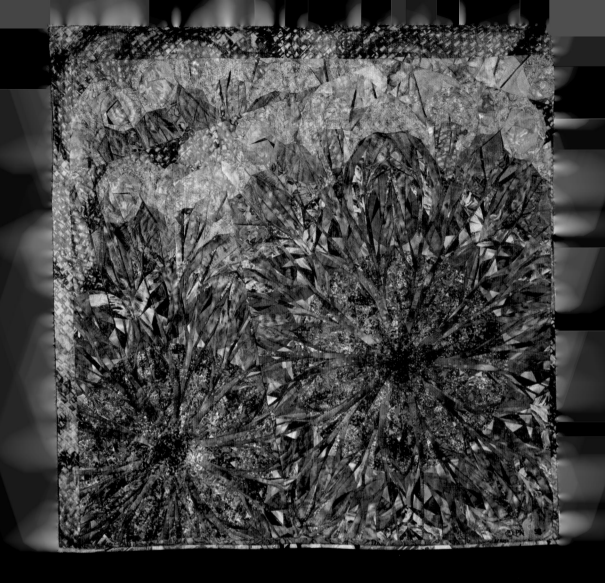

KALEIDOSCOPIC XIX:
TULIPS IN THE
COURTYARD BELOW

1998, Bronx, NY

36″ × 36″

Textiles: Cottons, silk

Techniques: Machine pieced, hand quilted

Quick. Make a second quilt measuring a yard square, fulfilling the *Yardworks* theme. My mind pounced on an image: me, staring out my kitchen window, nine stories up, in early May, in early morning, coffee cup in hand, rallying for another vigilant day at my father's bedside. Through the sadness, glimmers of bright colors peeked through the not-yet-full foliage of the tree I looked down on, vying to refocus my attention. What were those flashes of red and violet? Startled from my thoughts, I took a minute of pleasure from fragments of tulips in the communal backyard.

The vague irregularity of odd-sided kaleidoscopes always catches my attention. But a design divided into an even number of divisions can be constructed much more easily than one with an odd number. In an even-number design, half of the triangles pieced together will form a straight edge, and I only sew straight lines. But, what if, instead of making ten identical wedges, I made five left-sided and five right-sided? Would the resulting image act as a five-sided, odd-numbered design, even though the underlying structure would be an even-numbered division of ten?

Out went the familiar central axis with identical elements repeated in the same position on either side. Instead, I mentally separated the 36° triangle into a left and a right, considering each its own entity. My plan was to create some motifs focused toward the left side and completely different ones directed to the right, conscious that elements along each of the triangle's sides would connect to their mirror image. For all intents and purposes, this strategy divided a 72° wedge into two.

Left 36°   Right 36°

 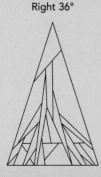

 + 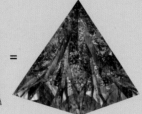 =

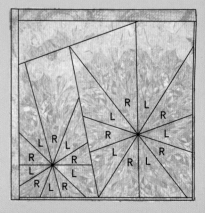

I first used a ten-sided design to create the illusion of a five-sided pentagon in *Kaleidoscopic X: Water from the Moon*, 1993.

KALEIDOSCOPIC XX:
ELEGANT AFTER MATHS

1999, Bronx, NY

61″ × 61″

Textiles: Cottons, silk by Pieces of Eight

Techniques: Machine pieced, hand quilted

W orking in a series provides time to revisit an idea, and time provides the clarity to see a familiar idea from a different point of view. This quilt has an underlying traditional pattern of 60° triangles set in seven horizontal rows. Every kaleidoscope is the same size, predetermined by the width of the rows. To make a scope seem smaller and float, like the kaleidoscope all the way to the right in rows 2 and 3, I simply finished the design short of the designated bottom and filled in the difference with background fabric. In this case, the size was eight inches, and the ground was four yards of a splendid silk, hand dyed by the late Dianne Smith.

Wanting a seamless effect, I worked cautiously with the silk, mapping out segments to be cut not contiguously but from dark to light, planning the darkest portion toward the bottom and getting lighter toward the right and top. This meant coordinating the placement of each scope in order to determine the color of background that would surround it. That color had to be introduced toward the base of the wedges. Once the layout is figured out, the wedges get pieced into rows, never into kaleidoscopes. It wasn't until Row 6 was sewn to Row 7 that the finished versions of the three bottom scopes were revealed.

My MO is to camouflage seams through fabric manipulation, to encourage an uninterrupted flow of design or color from one fabric patch to the next. As the eye moves around a kaleidoscope, elements appear in a regular and eventually anticipated order. After establishing a lulling, repetitive radial pattern, this quilt explores what happens when slight discrepancies interrupt the rhythm in some of the kaleidoscopes. My objective was to get the viewer to wonder why I dissolved the expected repetition.

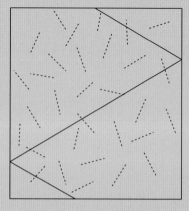

I quilted the body of the quilt with a user-friendly pattern of 1″-long discontinuous lines.

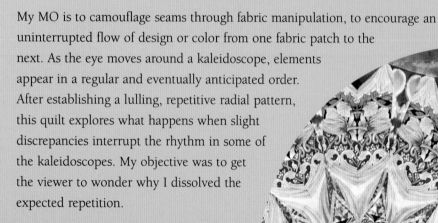

The colors were inspired by the kimono by Itchiku Kubota entitled Gaudi.

The interior border is the right and wrong side of a French silk from the 1950s, purchased in the Los Angeles garment district. Its doughnut-shaped motif inspired the hand quilting pattern around the edge.

The first time I used this layout in the series was in *Kaleidoscopic XII: Up Close and Far Away*, 1994.

To coax fluid silks into a cottonlike consistency that I can work with, I fuse featherweight interfacing to one side.

KALEIDOSCOPIC XXI:
THE THANK YOUR LUCKY
STAR MEMORIAL QUILT

2000, Bronx, NY

46″ × 45″

Textiles: Cottons, silk, hand-dyed cotton by Lunn Fabrics
and Quilt Tapestry Studio

Techniques: Machine pieced, hand quilted

From the collection of Ariel Nadelstern

To its maker, every quilt becomes a soft document, chronicling the events that took place during its evolution. In this case, what began as a requiem for one family member turned into a celebration of another loved one's survival.

The quilt begins simply as a centered six-sided image. Three long, straight seams dissect a big square, extending through the inner border pieced from an extraordinary piece of kimono silk. I had to figure out a way to handle the seamlines that broke up the silk frame. I chose to turn this disruption into a deliberate design element, interrupting the nuanced colors with skinny, dark slivers set at different angles. Now the long important seams that enabled me to sew it all together disappeared.

The pieced background is more complex than the main object. Laid-back stars pieced from the same three fabrics were patched together using a swirly patterned batik. I took advantage of the batik's repeating whorls by sometimes cutting the same figure from the right and the wrong side of the cloth to create a mirror image. The batik dye process renders printed patterns that are typically equally legible on both sides of the fabric; I simply ignored slight color shifts between the designated front and back. I organized the batik's wide range of color into an *ombré*, creating a transition from the pale yellow to dark steely gray. This added complexity carries the viewer's eye smoothly from one form to the next, and from the lightest colors in the upper left diagonally down toward the darkest shades at the bottom right.

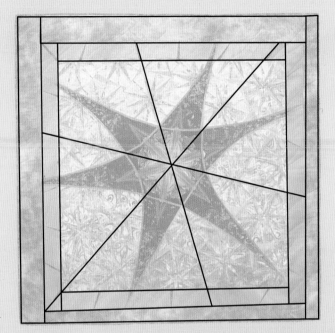

KALEIDOSCOPIC XXII:
ICE CRYSTALS

2000, Bronx, NY

41″ × 54″

Textiles: Cottons, silk

Techniques: Machine pieced, hand quilted

E very snow crystal that gently floats to earth is equally compelling. Our curiosity is aroused by this pure gem of nature, with its common hexagonal pattern and endless variety of structural details. The pieced snowflakes in this quilt are my attempt to translate into fabric a few of the over 6,000 photomicrographs made by W. A. Bentley of Jericho, Vermont, in the early 1900s and published by the American Meteorological Society in 1931.

Thanks to commercialism, most of us think of the snowflake as a visual paragon, a model of perfection. But how can a drifting ice crystal be perfect? It gets blown around in an active environment, flitting through clouds, colliding with its fellow crystals, acted upon by shifting winds and temperatures. Erasing nature's irregularities suits a craft sensibility that strives for perfection. But it is imperfection that renders snowflakes interesting, because of—not in spite of—their flaws. For a patchwork snowflake to step beyond pure technical prowess, I've learned to leave in some quirks and irregularities.

My techniques for piecing a snowflake are the same as for a kaleidoscope, but the design sensibility is different. I made six complete snowflakes, knowing from the start that a few would end up cropped, as if to suggest this snapshot is a segment of a larger storm. Only half of the snowflake visible along the left upper edge was ever made.

When I started making snowflakes in 1993, my intuition told me that in order for a bunch of fabrics to arrange themselves into the semblance of a snowflake, they had to be blue. The audience assumes that blues are cool colors and recognizes a chilly crystal thriving in a wintry mood. This quilt is filled with much more color than initially meets the eye. When I asked a group of fabric designers to catalog the colors, they found sapphire, indigo, royal blue, cobalt, ultramarine, denim, baby blue, pale blue, periwinkle, cerulean, iris, turquoise, and peacock. They also spotted blue-gray, pale gray, steel gray, slate, shale, pewter, tin, chromium, aluminum, mirror, smoke, and mauve.

To establish the illusion of a lacy three-dimensional snow-flake, a clear distinction needed to be set up between the object and background. The success of this effect hinged on the ability of the rich luxurious indigo, chosen as the common background fabric, to automatically combine with the backgrounds of the numerous prints into one continuous negative space.

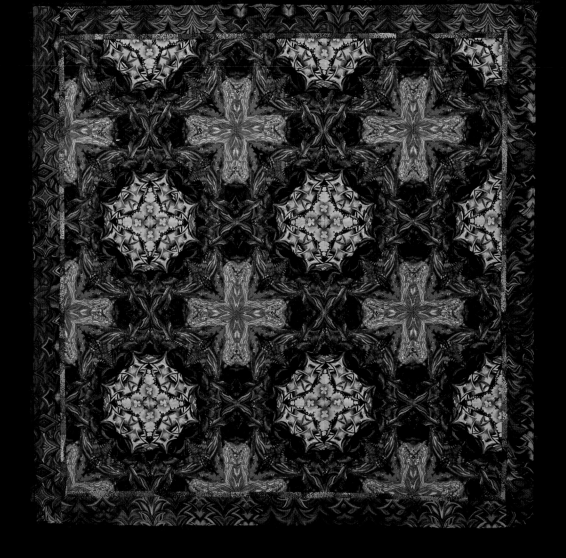

KALEIDOSCOPIC XXIII:

Cathy's Quilt

2001, Bronx, NY

37″ x 37″

Textiles: Cottons, silk

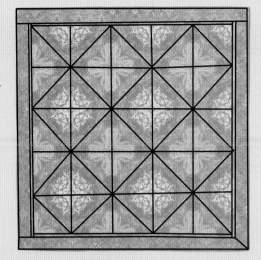

The image in a kaleidoscope is determined by the number and position of the mirrors and the angles at which they are placed. (The pattern and colors depend on the objects reflected in the mirrors). Since the invention of the kaleidoscope in 1816 by **Sir David Brewster**, two systems are used the most: the two-mirror system, which produces one central image, and the three-mirror system, which produces reflected images throughout the entire field of view. Perfectly symmetrical images are more difficult to achieve in a three-mirror kaleidoscope since there are three sets of angles that must be accurate. In the two-mirror system, only one angle is critical.

In the mid-nineties, a consummate kaleidoscope maker named Glenn Straub was asked to make a scope with an interior that looked like a quilt for a quilter with cancer. The result was an unusual, limited-edition kaleidoscope called *Kathy's Quilt*. Instead of the typical piece-of-pie shaped three-mirror system, this scope comprised a single isosceles right triangle, with angles set at 45°-45°-90°. The resulting image resembles a repeated square pattern, with the square actually being produced by two triangles, just as many quilt patterns are formed from half-square triangles. The 45°-45°-90° configuration presents a complex symmetry with repetitive patterns merging triangular and square shapes. According to Glenn, mirror precision is particularly crucial to achieve the desired effect. The slightest diversion from 45° or 90° will cause a breakdown of the symmetric structure. Irregularities get amplified the farther from the center of the pattern you go.

Up until this quilt, my kaleidoscopic journey explored the effects of two-mirror kaleidoscopes and was based on a wedge-shaped triangle. This time, the simple layout started with a 6″ half square pieced of fifteen patches, duplicated 25 times to the left and 25 times to the right. The result, overly balanced symmetry, was too much of a good thing and needed to be set off kilter to thrive.

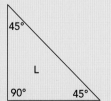 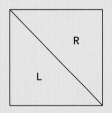 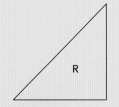

This quilt was made to honor the memory of my friend Cathy Rasmussen, who fought her long, brave fight against cancer armed with humor and a rare intelligence.

KALEIDOSCOPIC XXIV:
EBB & FLOW

2001, Bronx, NY

45″ × 59″

Textiles: Cottons, silk by Skydyes

Techniques: Machine pieced, hand quilted

An inherent consequence of working in a series is that each new piece suggests variations on a previous theme. Sometimes you get an opportunity to "correct" ideas that weren't well resolved, putting that dissatisfaction to positive use. Starting with the twelfth quilt, instead of images positioned against a neutral ground, a complex, animated background became a principal element in my quilts, effectively camouflaging the contours of the kaleidoscopic forms so they become ambiguous rather than sharply defined.

In traditional patchwork, contrasting colors are encouraged at the seams to emphasize the shape of the patch. Disguising the seams encourages an uninterrupted flow of color and shape from one patch to the next and compels the viewer to synthesize the components into a visual whole rather than analyze each element separately. This draws the audience physically closer to the quilt surface, inviting inspection of its organization. The intrigued viewer who gets involved hunting for seams bears witness to the quilt's inherent contradiction. What reads from a distance as a gentle wash of color and intensity is discovered to be a highly patched work.

I made a bunch of same-sized kaleidoscopes, challenging myself to mingle two color groups of my then-current fabric collection called Symmetry. Please don't laugh, but my objective was to explore a more muted, restrained palette. (I guess it's hard to see orange and think muffled and subdued.) The startling luminosity comes from the irregular streams of light provided by the silk in the border. The vaguely anemone-like structures are strip-pieced from silks (using large tracing paper templates) and help camouflage the long seams that ultimately sew the big patched-together segments together. The golden-yellow bricks in the border were cut as is out of a hideous upholstery-weight garment district find peppered with weird unrelated motifs.

This quilt was originally made to hang horizontally.

KALEIDOSCOPIC XXV:

IT's ABOUT TIME

2001, Bronx, NY

36″ x 36″

Textiles: Cottons, silk

Techniques: Machine pieced, hand quilted

T his piece is one of sixteen quilts created for *Time Squared*, the third
Manhattan Quilters Guild traveling exhibit. Working in their signature style,
some guild members chose a particular moment in time, others interpreted
the theme to depict an abstract concept of time; a few used the idea of squares
and grids, or referred to Times Square itself.

Me? I thought, "It's about time I tried something new."

Rather than my typical pie-slice sector, I drafted a 3″ × 30″ rectangular block
on graph paper and put my trust in symmetry. I pieced the skinny rectangle six
times, right side up, and, by flipping templates over, made six mirror-imaged
versions. When a left and right were sewn together, the patches along both long
seams connected to their mirror images, acting as if reflected and multiplying
into new, unique pathways. Whatever I did to one, I did to the eleven others—
except for the six inches along the top and bottom. That's where I
combined three colorways of an African batik in uneven
amounts, breaking up the symmetry before it could
become humdrum, directing the visual traffic
horizontally, using the darkest portions to
weigh the quilt down.

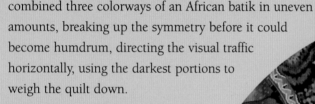

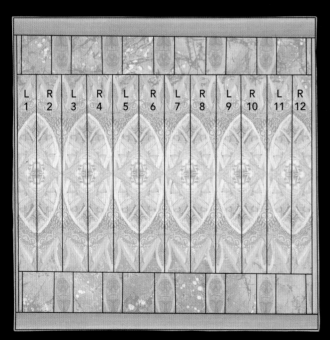

| L 1 | R 2 | L 3 | R 4 | L 5 | R 6 | L 7 | R 8 | L 9 | R 10 | L 11 | R 12 |

This quilt is based on a four-mirror rectangular system rather than a triangular system. The repeated images created are striped patterns, since the reflections move directionally up-down and right-left.

KALEIDOSCOPIC XXVI:
BIG RED CHORUS LINE

2002, Bronx, NY
81″ × 55½″
Textiles: Cottons

Inevitably, one quilt suggests another. This, my second exploration of a four-mirror system, pays homage to the effect known (in the kaleidoscope world) as a chorus line, suggesting that the pieces of glass are kicking their legs all at the same time.

Sometimes a design idea reveals itself in a sudden intuitive realization, like a glorious epiphany. Not this time. I got started on this quilt before I understood the big picture by building the blocks: five left-sided and five right-sided rectangles, each measuring 8″ × 50″, figuring these would add up to a pretty big quilt, and I like big. I realized I wanted to skew the pattern, but it wasn't until I met an oversized, painterly red stripe with lively, seemingly haphazard brush strokes that I found my happy ending. This wacky stripe was the right device at the right time, offering a strong but playful sense of movement, which is a good thing, because a quilt called *Big Red Chorus Line* shouldn't take itself too seriously.

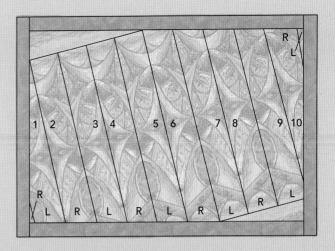

KALEIDOSCOPIC XXVII:
September 11, 2002

2002, Bronx, NY

42″ x 47″

Textiles: Commercial cottons and silks; specialty textiles created by Lunn Fabrics, Pieces of Eight, Skydyes, and Rebecca Yaffe

Techniques: Machine pieced by Paula Nadelstern; machine quilted by Jeri Riggs

The inevitable ruminations about the role of art and artist immediately after September 11, 2001, a crisis of unnerving proportion, led me to the conclusion that the creative process was futile. One year later, finishing this quilt in time for an exhibition, I reconsidered: creating beauty in a tumultuous world may be an act of optimism, an opportunity to shape my own spirituality.

This quilt began as a personal challenge: move out of my comfort zone and instill more contrast. Make something simultaneously fuzzy and detailed, structured and unpredictable. Draw on the seemingly paradoxical insight provided by the study of chaos: rich kinds of order arise spontaneously from the unplanned interaction of many simple things. To make this happen, I tried to free myself from a conventional sense of fabric orderliness, seeking a random quality.

I didn't like the finished version. It seemed like concentric but unrelated rings. After the piece was bound and quilted, I used black permanent marker to reinforce divisions and couched other lines with embroidery thread to highlight elements. I beaded the center for a more riveting focus.

Yes, that's velve

But the simple fix with the complex
result was a gold permanent marker
used to shade patches of mottled
olive green silk, causing this circle
of repeats to recede. For the first
time, this patchwork crammed with
an abundance of shading became
luminous and dimensional and
made sense.

KALEIDOSCOPIC XXVIII:
THE GREAT ROUND-UP

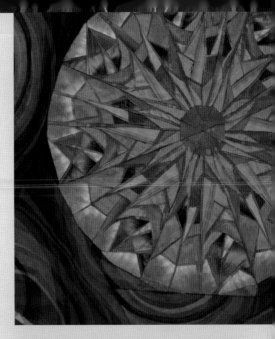

Someone once told me that plagiarizing yourself is the height of conviction. What was once innovation becomes a personal strategy, leading sometimes to imitation, other times to experimentation.

These scopes recycle a configuration first conceived in 1996 and used in *Kaleidoscopic XVI: More Is More*, alternating between two different wedges rather than repeating a single one. Only this time, I first made twelve different sets of $22\frac{1}{2}°$ wedges and then paired them up, two groups per scope, imagining that random matchmaking would convey a spontaneous quality imitating the chance interlinkings synonymous with kaleidoscopes.

The soul of this quilt can best be described by a clever phrase used by my closest friends: *semper tedium*. Essentially it means, when there is a hard way to do something, we'll find it. Case in point: the complex background was pieced from three different exquisitely hand-marbled silks. Not only was it like sewing eels (in spite of the fusible interfacing I added), there was no forgiving, reliable repeat to supply continuity of a form when the design called for it. And casting silk as a major player in a curved seam illusion was just plain tedious.

Quilters are often asked, "How long did it take?" Is there a right answer? Is shorter better? Does it make you more clever if you figured out how to race through the process in record time and now you can get on with life's so-called important stuff? Or is longer better because it shows you are industrious and persevering? Sometimes, when one of my labor-intensive quilts provokes this question, I answer, "My whole life." It sounds facetious and glib, but it is, in fact, the truth.

This layout was inspired by an ornate screen I once saw in a posh NYC shop filled with vintage urban stuff. Later that day, I scribbled my memory on a paper napkin and hung it on my bulletin board, where it remained for years. That's why I originally conceived this quilt as a vertical piece. But a couple of years later, I consented to hanging it horizontally because of space constraints and liked the composition better.

The fabric filling the large curlicue along the quilt's bottom edge is burgundy-colored cotton. The stream of concentric rings bubbling across this surface was cut from the marbled silk and hand appliquéd in place.

KALEIDOSCOPIC XXIX:
HOW TO PIECE A SPIRAL

2003, Bronx, NY

12″ x 12″

Textiles: Cottons

Techniques: Machine pieced, hand quilted

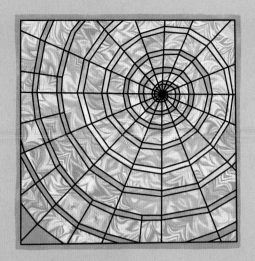

During a trip to Japan, I found myself appreciating and appraising the design sensibility of graceful, seamless spirals, including the uninterrupted sand patterns raked in dry gardens known as *karesansui*. I sat, one tourist among many, mesmerized by the simple arrangements of a few stones and swirls of sand. Contemplating this aesthetic, it came to me that I had the skills and desire to form a spiral from a fabric with patterns printed in a straight line, letting it follow itself around and around a fixed center.

This spiral's underlying shape is an octagon. It's composed of two fabrics, with a third black fabric used in the lower left corner and binding. The motifs curve and coil around and don't appear to be interrupted by seams. Each template is used only once. A simplified explanation of this construction strategy is in Continuous Templates, on page 109.

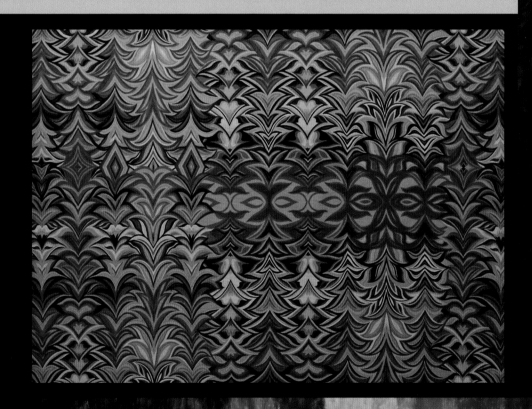

KALEIDOSCOPIC XXX:
TREE GRATE, 53RD AND 7TH

2004, Bronx, NY

58½″ × 51½″

Textiles: Cottons, silk

Techniques: Machine pieced, hand quilted

A tree grate integrates trees into the cityscape, suppressing weeds while allowing pedestrian traffic over the tree planting area. I'm a born and bred New Yorker. How many times had I stepped on these urban accessories before the day I looked down and instantly recognized the shape of my next quilt?

My fascination was more lyrical than practical. I wasn't aiming to freeze-frame the image, but to capture and convey its nature and have fun with color. Variations within the interlocking circles point to the handiwork of an anonymous craftsman. I used a special stash of high-end cottons printed in allover patterns accumulated over time in the NYC garment district. I enjoyed organizing them into a subtle blend that gently shifts the eye from the center out. Although the fabrics are vibrant on their own, in this context the black outlines appear suspended above a muted ground, except for bursts of energetic, attention-grabbing color balanced in the borders.

Photo: Robin Schwalb

On my last day in Tokyo, I lucked into a fabric store tucked into a neighborhood known for its flamboyant temple. Imagine my glee when the sign over the roll of kimono silk I coveted turned out to say 50 percent off. It was approximately fourteen inches wide by twelve yards. This stunning silver-to-black silk ombré makes nimble visual transitions, first spinning around an inner circle, then setting up an alternating give-and-take rhythm leading in and out of what is, to me, a kaleidoscope.

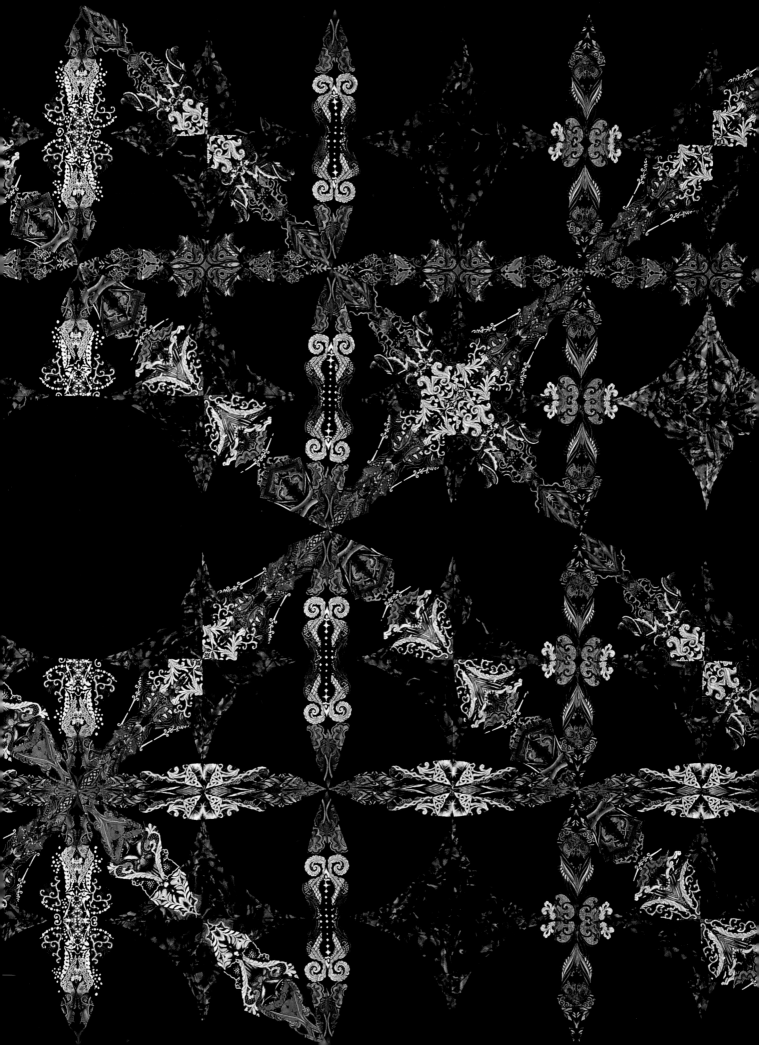

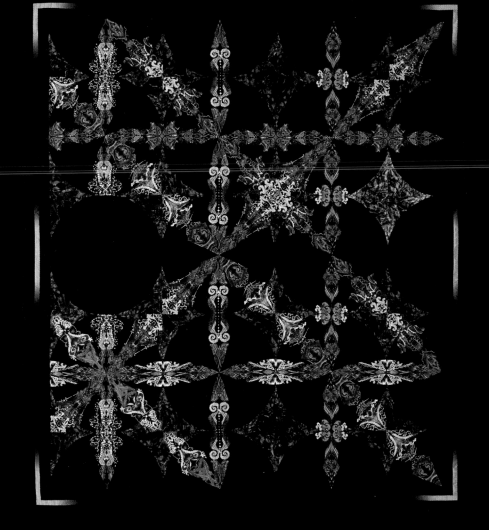

KALEIDOSCOPIC XXXI:
THE OTHER SIDE
OF THE CIRCLE

2006, Bronx, NY

63˝ × 72½˝

Textiles: Cottons, silk

Techniques: Machine pieced, hand quilted

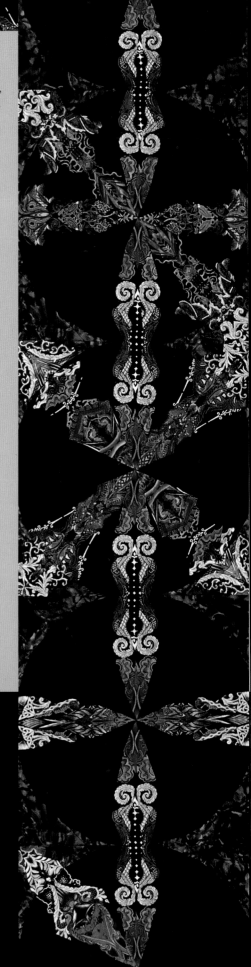

W hen you work in a series, the questions you ask yourself get more complex, while the answers get simpler. A kaleidoscope functions like a circle. Structurally it may be a geometric shape, but to uncover its artistic soul, you have to think of it as a radial design. This time I wondered, how can I use the same structure to make the eye travel in straight lines before it discovers the circles? I knew it would work in practice, but could it work in theory? Can the negative space and the lines both become the focal point?

As it often is, an octagon was my foundation. The quilt was built from squares; the squares were built from eight wedges and four corner triangles. But this time, the centers are not kaleidoscopic. Identical wedges are atypically positioned tip to bottom, bottom to tip, tip to bottom, and so on, forming lines that command attention while they crisscross the quilt. The explosion of energy expected from the center is not there. Mirror imaging occurs when two identical triangles bump bottoms or combine in attention-grabbing corners.

I chose a common ground, returning again (albeit thirteen quilts later) to basic black, which efficiently coaxes the dark backgrounds of the controlled, restricted palette to recede into communal negative space. I'm used to stuffing my wedges from edge to edge with pattern, but this time I learned to cautiously confine motifs within a narrow path centered in the triangle. The result is lacy intricacy floating on top, reminiscent of snowflakes.

I'm not sure what this quilt looks like to anyone else. It probably doesn't say kaleidoscope to anyone but me. I've known for a while that no matter what my quilts look like, my personal design vocabulary, gleaned through the eyepiece of a kaleidoscope, will take the journey with me.

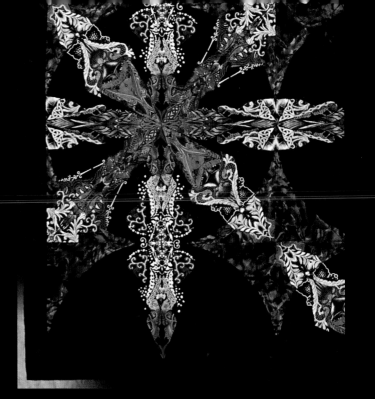

This is the second quilt to use the kimono silk with its silver-to-black ombré. Because kimono silk is only 14″ wide, many seams were needed to achieve the total length needed for this radiant effect showcased in the borders.

The underlying structure is the traditional nineteenth century kaleidoscope quilt.

KALEIDOSCOPIC XXXII:
MY BROOKLYN BRIDGE

2006, Bronx, NY

36˝ × 36˝

Textiles: Cottons, silk

Techniques: Machine pieced, hand appliquèd
and couched, long arm and hand quilted

The classic photo of this East River landmark is an homage to symmetry, the view peeking through a mesh of its iconic web of cables anchored to Gothic arches and stone towers. When faced with an assignment to create a 36″-square quilt relating in some way to ideas of texture and the city, this image seemed made to show off the bilaterally symmetrical patterns I like to play with. But what textiles possessed the gravitas needed to fill up the vast sky, proportionally half the quilt? *This* was where I could introduce my signature style. Now was the time to indulge in a black and white kaleidoscopic sky.

But would an opulently patterned bridge disappear against an equally decorative sky? The only way to know was to see. That meant first making an eight-sided kaleidoscope with wedges potentially long enough to fill the 32″-wide sky. But since too much symmetry can seem mundane, I placed the kaleidoscope off center. To be on the safe side, four wedges needed to be longer than 18″ (22″ long), one even longer, and three 12″ long or less. Eventually they'd get evenly sliced into a straight edge. Once that was made, I could answer the question opening this paragraph: No. The towers needed to be built from simpler material. To me simple meant four colorways (all unlikely choices for a bridge) of a textured cotton I designed to evoke Japanese dyed *shibori*. The black-to-silver kimono silk is used in the border and the walkway.

I layered the web of cables by hand couching, building up thin twists of cords and threads until I was satisfied with the degree of contrast against the patchwork. The towers are hand appliquéd to the quilt. A kind shop owner gave me, an utter novice and Luddite, a chance to use her store's long arm machine when I was teaching in Oklahoma City.

This quilt was made for the fourth Manhattan Quilters Guild traveling exhibit titled METROTEXTURAL.

KALEIDOSCOPIC XXXIII:
Shards

2007, Bronx, NY

57″ x 64³⁄₄″

Textiles: Cottons

Techniques: Machine pieced, hand and machine quilted

A s an art quilter working in a series, I continually reconnect to my bank of quilt making memories. I reap what I sew, harvesting ideas and techniques planted in preceding quilts. For example:

- Turning straight rows of intricate, patterned cloth into circular bands of concentric rings

- Matchmaking mirror images into seamless connections to mimic uninterrupted continuity

- Choosing highly contrasting colors between adjacent rings to allow the eye to see the circular shape

Another ongoing design element explored in my quilts, reminiscent of a traditional quilt pattern, is that a definite focal point is not always required to create a successful design. Not having a primary focal point doesn't mean the viewer will be confused and not know where to look. Her eye will take her where it wants to go. The ordered quality of unity balances the lively quality of variety.

This quilt took a long time, bound eighteen months after the first stitch. It is built of kaleidoscopic structures cracked into fragments and cemented back together by irregularly stripped-on silver-gray "grout", another idea attesting to the influence of earlier quilts. I learned to machine quilt for the first time, using a walking foot to stitch closely spaced lines on the highly seamed grout. I intended to sew with a silver thread similar to the fabric color, but I picked up the wrong spool the minute I started and was then committed to the textured effect created by a darker gray.

I couldn't figure out how to proceed via a hypothetical thought experiment. Instead, figuring out the process meant physically making identical triangles, piecing them together, and then imagining the product splintered into fragments like a shattered ceramic plate. I wanted to convey the illusion that a cracked scope is grouted back together along its broken edges, and the shards sharing this communal junction were originally from the same wedge. Realize that to give this impression, I needed to make an additional wedge to compensate for the part of the shard that disappeared into the seam allowance. I started in the upper left corner, and over the next year, eventually drafted the entire diagram to scale, making tracing paper templates to fit units together.

The palette can best be described by adjectives rather than colors: *luminous, sumptuous, lavish, thoughtful.* A lot of thought went into these choices.

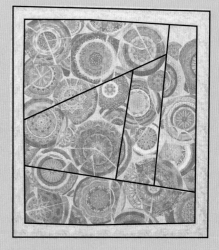

Remember, there is no curved piecing in this quilt; it is constructed solely of straight lines.

At the same time that it was difficult to sustain the fussiness of this arrangement (deciding every few inches if the part I was working on should continue, shift direction, or jarringly disconnect), the constant options fed my curiosity. I was committed to completing this quilt however long it took. In fact, quilters with their drawers full of UFOs (jargon for unfinished objects, referring to the propensity of most quilters to have multiple projects going on at one time) will find it interesting that I work on only one quilt at a time. I credit the switch to a single kaleidoscopic quilt from start to finish as one of the major markers on my path from amateur to artist.

the
ARTFUL KALEIDOSCOPE

Choosing a theme like kaleidoscopes means working with a recognizable subject. Although dependent on the techniques and materials of quiltmaking, the content must conform to our sense of a kaleidoscope. So what, exactly, is that?

ka-lei-do-scope *n.*

1. A tube-shaped optical instrument that is rotated to produce a succession of symmetrical designs by means of mirrors reflecting the constantly changing patterns made by bits of glass at one end of the tube.

2. A constantly changing set of colors.

3. A series of changing phases or events. [Greek *kalos*, beautiful + *eidos*, form]

There it is. Our role as kaleidoscope quilter defined: we must convey a physical sense of change and chance. Throw in luminosity (because kaleidoscopes rely on the reflection of light rays from the mirrors), intricate details (because the mirrors conjure up complex images brimming with interlaced patterns), spontaneity and transience (reminiscent of the chance interlinkings and seemingly endless possibilities synonymous with kaleidoscopes), and we've got our work cut out. Oh, and don't forget the symmetry. Put it all together and behold the intangible: *a glimpse of infinity.*

Please. Read the sections that follow in the order in which they are presented. Approach this book as you would a book of fiction. After all, I made up most of this stuff. Even though it's more of a howtodoit than a whodunit, skip around and you might miss a vital nugget of vocabulary or a piece of the plot.

You're going to have to trust me; I teach this approach a lot. I know where it gets inevitably tedious, where lengthy explanations pay off, where a picture is worth the proverbial thousand words. I know that some of you appreciate abstract musings and others do not. This is an art form that is filled with nuance, and I resist oversimplifying the process. So I have a lot to say. That's a bad thing? At least I'm not like that passive-aggressive cook who offers the recipe, then leaves one thing out. I am, however, known to go off on tangents at the slightest provocation. Here, then, is my compromise: every so often, I'll drop hints about a Paula-ism, and when we meet for lunch, you can ask me about it. Otherwise, I could go on for pages and pages, and that would make my publisher's hair uncurl.

Before we get to the practical step-by-step and set your kaleidoscope in motion, give me a chance to convey my idiosyncratic strategies about piecing and designing. Distilled from twenty years of complex quiltmaking, this is the substance that knocks the traditional nineteenth-century pattern known as Kaleidoscope into the twenty-first.

Happy Scrappy Kaleidoscope, work in progress by Marti Michell.

Photo by Bread and Butter Studio, Atlanta, Georgia.

MY PIECE POLICY

Designing a kaleidoscope is a collaboration between me and my fabric stash. I don't draw random lines on the diagram and then choose fabrics to fill in the blanks. Sewing lines and templates follow my fabric choices, not the other way around. The objective is to create a design that sews together successfully. For me, this means an intricate pattern that fits together easily, has no hidden hurdles, and gives the appearance that I know how to sew really well.

Here's my strategy: for each kaleidoscope I make, I'm only going to draft one full-size triangle on graph paper. This diagram functions as my work-in-progress blueprint tempered by my palette of fabric—a detailed plan revealing every sewing line. In fact, *only* sewing lines are allowed on the diagram so that I don't risk interpreting stray lines as seamlines. I know it isn't easy for those not used to mechanical drawing to adopt the habit of marking every decision on the diagram. But this is the step that provides a design plan, explains the relationships between all the patches, and ensures they will fit together. Give it a chance.

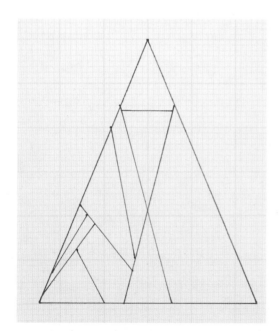

Draw every line in pencil so that it can be edited when needed.

This may sound counterintuitive, but although I'm using graph paper with a grid, the outlines of the patches aren't dictated by the grid. Patches tend to be irregular shapes with three, six, or even more sides (the amount is irrelevant). Together they form a network of straight seamlines imposed on the graph but not shaped or suggested by the grid. Why then, you ask, do I bother to work on a grid? Because having the identical grid on the graph paper and transparent plastic templates lets me use both as if they are rulers. The grid also disciplines symmetry. These are really good perks. Not only can I measure fabric motifs, I can transfer these measurements from fabric to template to diagram. This relationship (drum roll, please) is the design-technique interface.

I never complete a mock-up of a single wedge before starting to sew the others. Instead, I sew identical units at the same time, using an assembly line approach. Whatever I do for one wedge, I follow up immediately for all of its mates. By the time the end is in sight, all of the wedges are at an identical stage of completion. It's a remarkably efficient piecing arrangement, and not knowing what it's going to look like in the end keeps me engrossed every step of the way.

As the design evolves, the patches are sewn together into irregularly shaped units that combine into bigger sections. Eventually, the diagram may look complex enough to launch something into outer space, but if you can identify straight lines partitioning the units, the final fit is not unlike a Nine-Patch. Three criteria are crucial for successful piecing:

■ Every sewing line must be straight.

■ The chosen angle, for example, 45°, must be maintained along the "legs" of the triangle.

■ The "i" word is to be avoided.

The dreaded "i" word is *inset*. An inset is a corner. I never sew into a corner, aptly defined by Webster as an awkward place from which escape is difficult, because then I'd have to sew my way out of it, six or eight flawless times. It may be possible to make a few, maybe even several, respectable insets, but at least one is bound to malfunction, selfishly skewing its neighboring patches along with it. When a bunch of decisions spontaneously construct to form an inset, don't accept this penciled setup as inevitable. You are never limited to one specific solution. You put the lines there, you can take them away.

My usual response is to turn a potential Y-seam (another name for an inset) into what I call an X-seam. This alternate solution provides practically the same effect and pieces together neatly along a straight line. It offers an opportunity to arrange patches at different levels instead of having them all end horizontally. Plus, Patch X in the diagram doesn't meet itself, so it's a great spot for a pseudosymmetrical fabric. Patch Y (Left) can be made up of one fabric or ten, but in the end it gets treated as a single unit and is sewn to X. Patch Y (Right) gets sewn to Patch 1.

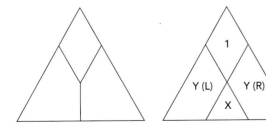

I also avoid bulky construction sites by circumventing a multitude of seams whenever possible. When I see three or more sewing lines about to crash into the same destination, I reroute the drafted lines to avoid a collision. Of course, there are times when this kind of detour isn't possible or desirable. There are also times when rethinking the design because of these considerations becomes a creative springboard, suggesting "what if" scenarios that take the design someplace even better.

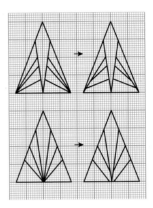

Redraft sewing lines to disperse a crowd of seams.

Design a little, piece a little, design a little more. I tend to stay absorbed in the act of designing through two to four fabric choices, at which point my mind's eye overloads. That's when I stop, make sure every decision is measurable, and transfer it to the graph paper diagram. I can't continue designing without an accurate, up-to-date blueprint. What is already designed inspires the next sequence of decision making. After that, I pick a task that fits my prevailing mood. Chances are I'll make the templates needed to execute these choices and mark and cut all of the patches. But if I'm in a flow state—the name for those glorious moments when you're so energized by the task at hand that time seems immaterial—then I might stay there and design more. In this case, I'll cut out only one of each patch to use for reference and dive into another string of decision making.

After a bout of designing, I check the graph paper diagram to see if the decisions I just made lead to an arrangement that can be sewn together. If yes, I sew all of the same components at the same time. I don't make a mock-up first. Other times, it's apparent that a few more patches need to be determined before the sewing arrangement is inset-free.

My Design Strategies

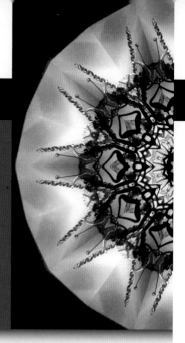

Before I tell you how I do what I do, let me say that it always takes longer than you'd expect to design something good. Designing doesn't proceed along a straight line. It goes forward and back and wanders around in all directions. It's not always a fun place to be. Sometimes the aha! moments arrive unbidden via cartoonish light bulbs. Other times, you just have to hunker down and coax inspiration. When I've plodded away in an unproductive place way too long, the act of doing something different, of focusing on one small task, works to calm me down and set me back on course.

Typically, when I am stuck, I dive headfirst into piles of fabrics. It's kind of a Zen thing. Enlightenment is attained by pretending to organize, when really I'm hunting and gathering. I grab the fabrics that ask to be in the current project even if they seem like unlikely guests. They've touched some intuitive link in my brain, and like a CSI agent, I consider it my job to investigate every option. At least, that's how I do it. Think for a minute. You use problem-solving skills every day. You know your own method to rev your juicing skills into high gear.

Be patient. Don't accept a solution if you don't like it. (If you don't like it now, you won't like it when the quilt is finished.) It takes a long time to make something good. In fact, it takes all kinds of time: looking time, musing time, auditioning time, screwing up time, constructing and deconstructing time. Give yourself the luxury of time to harvest those valuable "what if" ideas. It's a terrible thing to waste a great idea, the kind that matures over time as the project develops.

Seemingly Seamless

MY CONCEPT. In traditional patchwork, the visual key to the design is contrasting colors at the seams. A Nine-Patch, for example, features a single shape—the square—laid out in a checkerboard effect. The quiltmaker chooses fabrics with contrasting colors or values in order to create a distinct, obvious line between patches 1 and 2.

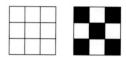

Nine-Patch block

My MO is often the opposite: to camouflage seams and create seemingly seamless connections. This encourages an uninterrupted flow of design or color from one patch to the next. Instead of sharp, straight edges defining shapes, the result is a smooth transition from patch to patch, with the illusion that there are no seams at all. As far as I'm concerned, patches are vehicles for carrying intricate, complex fabric onto the quilt top. I want their shapes to be ignored, not highlighted.

Don't get me wrong. It's not that I never want to use a seamline to create an area of contrast. Rather, I plan these areas deliberately and judiciously because I am aware of the role they play in the design. Fabricating an elaborate kaleidoscope with interlaced patterns means disguising the underlying geometry that ultimately allows you to sew it all together.

I define a viable quilt as one that compels the viewer to witness its inherent contradiction. What reads from a distance as an integrated whole is discovered—up close—to be a highly patched work. When "seamless" techniques are used, the visual whole draws the audience physically closer to the quilt surface to hunt for the seams and stitches. In my opinion, if the viewer is content to see a quilt only from far away or only up close, the quilt is not successful.

Detail of a pieced snowflake

APPLYING THE CONCEPT. In order to invent seamless connections, you have to free yourself from a conventional sense of patchwork. Often the trick is to choose a fabric based on the color in its background, the color that will land right along the seamline and connect to the neighboring patch's background color. That position, right at the seam, turns out to be crucial. When the color that functions as the ground is pieced to a patch with a similar color at the seamline, the seamline between disappears. Instead of focusing on the patchwork lines, we see patterns in the fabric advance and float against a receding common ground. This illusion is easier to pull off with dark rather than light backgrounds because colors like black, indigo, forest green, and wine tend to blend smoothly into each other. Tones of beige and white don't have the same color dexterity.

That's why, when I hunt for the next fabric, the search is based on the relationship I want to establish with the previous one. Sometimes I want to continue the mood and look for a subtle effect created by minimal contrast. Other times, I want to define clearly where one patch ends and the next begins. I find terms like sharp or harsh, mild or minimal useful for defining degrees of contrast. This vocabulary focuses my options and directs the search.

So in a nutshell, what is the kaleidoscope quilter's quandary? To Contrast or Not to Contrast, that is the question. Whether it is better to use distinct colors and end up with an obvious seam that creates a visible line or whether to disguise the seam by placing similar colors at the seamline. It's as simple as that.

Having established that the diagram must be rectilinear, meaning its internal forms have straight edges, let me reiterate that I don't want to emphasize its linear nature. My earliest scopes reveal a mundane design tendency I want to warn you about. If you cause a visible line to travel straight across the entire wedge, from one side to the other, this line runs parallel to the outer skeletal edge of the final hexagon, octagon, or whatever-gon and becomes a visual clue. Since our eyes tend to follow a line, we trail this one as it bends around the geometric shape, forming a smaller shape within. Granted, this formation may appear in an actual kaleidoscope, and it is *de rigueur* for a snowflake, but, as far as I'm concerned, it's not a kaleidoscope at the peak of its performance.

Three early scopes, 1988

COMMON GROUND

MY CONCEPT. Here is an alternate way to think about seamless connections. Consider a piece of patterned fabric as if it is a dimensional object and make a distinction between what is figure (pattern) and what is ground. The principle of figure/ground is one of the most basic laws of perception, referring to the ability to distinguish elements based upon contrast.

The idea is to set up the illusion of one continuous negative space by causing the backgrounds of neighboring patches to visually combine into a common ground. This sets up a visual hierarchy. Pattern not perceived as background is distinguished as the main subject. Floating on the surface, these figures merge into the composition's focal point. Some of the most elegant kaleidoscopes have a lot of important negative space.

APPLYING THE CONCEPT. Build from the ground up. As a kaleidoscope rotates, colored objects tumble into arbitrary but symmetrical patterns isolated against a solid black background. Fabricate this quintessential quality by first choosing an allover background fabric and then collect fabrics with similar-colored backgrounds. The success of this effect hinges on the ground color, so pick an easy-to-get color rather than an esoteric one.

Most of my quilts don't sit against plain or black grounds. Often a complex, allover fabric instigates a gleam in my mind's eye. In these cases, rather than a lacy effect right through the scopes, I'm usually concerned with camouflaging the contours of the kaleidoscopic forms so they appear as if they were appliquéd on a continuous whole cloth. I audition similarly colored allover cottons by placing snippets on top of the intended background fabric. If they disappear in this context, I can use them to visually "continue" the background fabric in the pieced scopes.

Decide if you want the audience to differentiate the figure effortlessly or if you'd prefer some ambiguity. Either is a reasonable design choice. If your objective is the former, reduce the level of distraction caused by the ground. Choose motifs separated entirely from the ground either by obvious outlines or sharp contrasts.

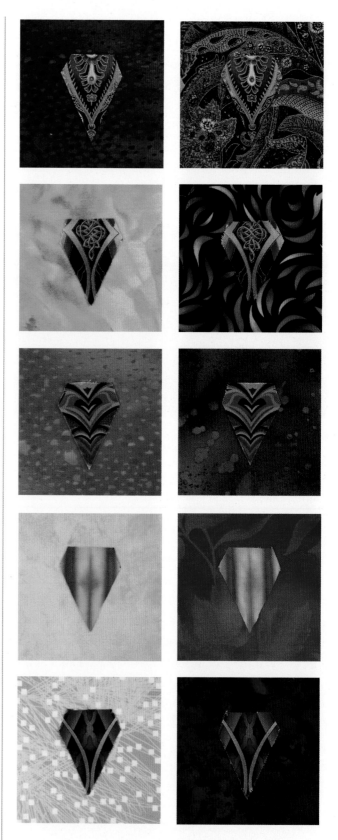

Left column: Shapes are sharp and distinct when viewed against a contrasting ground.

Right column: The printed motifs are more prominent than the patchwork shapes.

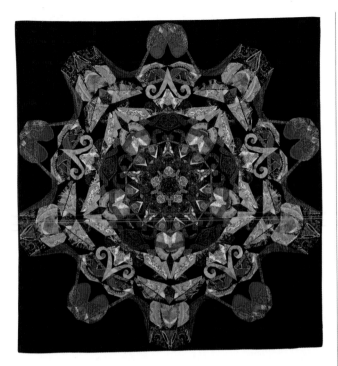

Kaleidoscopic X: Water from the Moon, 1993, 52″ × 53″. The multitude of background fabrics connect into continuous negative space, organizing and defining the shape of the kaleidoscope.

Although the backgrounds must be similarly colored, the figures don't need to be related by palette at all. In fact, this is how you can instill the unpredictable, unrestrained profusion of color that is synonymous with a kaleidoscope. The colors released by individual fabrics don't touch each other, the backgrounds they sit on do.

THE BUTTERFLY EFFECT

MY CONCEPT. Here is a painless way to conceptualize symmetry. Imagine a butterfly. It has two wings and what I unscientifically call a "belly." A symmetrical pattern will have a similar structure: two wings filled with patterns that are each other's mirror image and a belly (usually an itty-bitty motif), where one wing of fabric connects to the other.

APPLYING THE CONCEPT. If you're having trouble figuring out if a fabric print is symmetrical, start with the belly. In other words, look for an imaginary center line down the middle of a motif, the position where the pattern divides into right and left halves. Check to see if the pattern on one side of the line is the mirror image of the pattern on the other side of the line. A design is considered to be

mirror imaged when it can be superimposed on itself by bending it in half and flipping it over.

The gussied-up term for the butterfly effect is bilateral symmetry because it is formed of two sides, like the human body. Grownups refer to the belly of a symmetrical design as the central axis, the axis of symmetry, or the axis of reflection.

 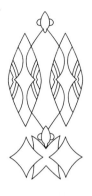

This symmetrical print illustrates the butterfly effect.   Outline drawing of the motif

SEA FOAM

MY CONCEPT. Why, in those glorious moments when we're lucky enough to find ourselves on a beautiful, sandy beach, do we gaze, mesmerized by the sea and think, "I could stare at this for hours." My theory? The staccato rhythm of foaming whitecaps compels the eyes to move around in a very satisfying way, searching for the next frothy swell. For some reason, the eternal ebb and flow of white meringues against a dark shimmering sea is simultaneously stimulating and soothing.

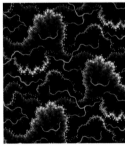

APPLYING THE CONCEPT. This discussion is about how to introduce that same lively brightness onto the flat surface of a quilt. Don't assume that using a light-colored fabric will do the trick. A light fabric placed next to a dark one will cause a blatant line of contrast, which will form a clunky patchwork shape, stopping the visual motion and disappointing you. If you want to shed light onto your quilt, find fabrics with luminous, light-colored motifs that stand out against appropriately colored backgrounds, meaning a background similar in color to the background of the patch next to it.

Again, the effect is based on a figure-ground relationship. Choose light-colored patterns splattered like randomly tossed confetti or churning like mermaid's breath or snaking like a sinuous echo. These will rise from the quilt surface the way sea foam flits on top of cresting waves. It's your chance to both lighten up and energize your scope.

MULTIPLICITY

MY CONCEPT. A kaleidoscope functions like a radial design because all the elements develop symmetrically around a common central point. A radial design directs the viewer's attention into the important center, the primary focal point. The eye travels around the design, making connections between recurring motifs and searching for secondary focal points and accents. Eventually, the central element draws the viewer's attention back to the center.

APPLYING THE CONCEPT. The whole is always greater than the sum of the parts. What you see in one single triangle is not what you get in the multiplied sum. The patches along the side seams of the pie-slice wedge connect to their mirror images and act as if reflected, multiplying into new, unique pathways. There is an air of abracadabra as the last seam is stitched, because effects more wonderful than you imagined occur. You get to be both the one who makes the magic and the one who is surprised.

Palette of fabrics used in the block

The finished block

A single 45° wedge

CHAOS THEORY

MY CONCEPT. If you haven't witnessed the magic firsthand, I know it's hard to visualize the final product based on a single wedge. You probably think I can predict the outcome, when really and truly, I can't. The difference between you and me is that (1) I trust in symmetry and (2) I know it is possible to create a pattern that is so overly coordinated and agreeable that the result offers visual boredom rather than satisfaction. Symmetry has two faces. It can be forceful and active, but too much can be bland and predictable. A true kaleidoscope is a complicated structure unified by its repetitive patterns. The ordered quality of unity balances the lively quality of variety.

APPLYING THE CONCEPT. Into every wedge, add a little chaos. A motif that seems awkward and unrelated in a single wedge will be well accepted in the finished product when it's peppered identically through the design. I rely heavily on the unifying element of repetition. A dash of something unexpected becomes a pulsating punctuation point due to its identical placement from wedge to wedge, reinforcing a visual rhythm.

If the end is in sight and you're not really worried about a couple of patches that seem odd and out of place, my advice is to go back and add more. I advocate audacity.

VISUAL MOTION

MY CONCEPT. The most effective kaleidoscopic designs create the illusion of motion. In our role as kaleidoscope constructors, we are concerned with two kinds of movement. The first is a visual sensation caused by the movement of the viewer's eye. Luckily for us, radial balance automatically activates this design element by establishing a rhythm based on recurring motifs. The repetitive flow of shapes and color carries the design across the seamlines from wedge to wedge. As the eye moves around, elements reappear in a regular, and eventually anticipated, order.

The second kind of motion to consider is a physical impression of change—not a manic sense of speed but rather a kaleidoscope's signature sensation: the constant and inevitable metamorphosis from one design into the next, resulting in a marked or complete change of character. There is no beginning or end.

APPLYING THE CONCEPT. The goal is to inject a feeling of motion into an otherwise static image. You can't predict the final and exact pathway of the viewer's eye, but you might influence the result by introducing accents.

Visual rhythm is based on repetition and instills a dynamic quality. The repetition of identical motifs causes the eye to leap from element to repeated element. Depending on the fabrics and motifs used, the pace and flow of this movement can range from a smooth, graceful undulation to a peppy, punchy march. There is a corresponding emotional response in the viewer.

THE IMPORTANCE OF BEING A DETAIL

MY CONCEPT. With the type of template making I'm going to teach you, you could center a complete cat face in a patch—but would you want to? It turns out that when mirror imaging is concerned, a known entity ends up looking like the same old, same old. Giving the audience a chance to recognize something identifiable slows down the visual action and kills the gestalt. A cropped image, on the other hand, multiplied many times, yields a unique, imaginative bit of intricacy that never existed before. The effect is unexpected, more spontaneous, and less manufactured. In fact, Charles Karadimos, a consummate kaleidoscope maker, considers the magic lost if the viewer can recognize the objects in his kaleidoscopes.

APPLYING THE CONCEPT. It's more in keeping with the kaleidoscope character for the audience to see a part rather than a whole motif. It conveys the illusion that one free-falling item has arbitrarily landed behind another and, if you keep watching, it may disappear entirely or be revealed even more. When you can describe a two-dimensional layout of fabric patches in these terms, you know you have conveyed a sense of depth, the impression that one object is in front of another.

Remember, a little bit goes a long way. Whatever is seen in one wedge is seen sixteen times if it lands off the center axis and eight times if it sits on it. Every patch located along the wedge's side seam is bound to bump into itself sixteen times.

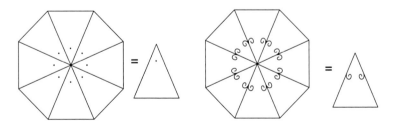

If this adds up to too much, whack some off and add something different, something that contrasts. This isn't the occasion for a seamless connection because a similar-looking fabric will visually attach to the original patch, putting it right back where it started.

Original version of Kaleidoscope B.
Motif lines up too perfectly.

Auditioning 8 more possibilities along the seams.
For final version, see page 120.

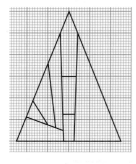

The original diagram.

The viewer's eye doesn't mind if it has to jump across a patch to make a connection between a pair of intricate, mirror-imaged twins. In fact, it appreciates working harder. A good example of this compelling disconnect are the luminous golden chevrons in Kaleidoscopic A, page 118. Visual motion feels good; it's lively and interesting. It seems contrived when everything lines up just so,

recreating entire figures—as if you actually had enough time to plan *and* measure *and* cut *and* sew. The perception of these many actions slows time down. If you're getting the idea that an essential element in a kaleidoscopic design is the illusion of fast, fleeting, agile time, you're on the right track.

THE POINT SYSTEM

MY CONCEPT. Patchwork etiquette favors distinct, well-matched points. But unconventional shapes are more in line with a kaleidoscope-inspired design, simulating the spontaneity and randomness synonymous with kaleidoscopes. Besides, it's difficult to match and stitch thin, acute angles accurately. Here are two solutions:

- Reshape severe points into more user-friendly forms, as shown in this scope by Knapp Studio. Points don't have to come to points to read as points.

- Accept that it is okay for points to join together unevenly. Irregular stabs of color enhance the design, perceived as pulsating momentary vibrations.

APPLYING THE CONCEPT. Evaluate every fussy point. Does it really have to be a precise barbed tip to enhance the design? Sometimes the answer is yes, like when reshaping a point into a nonpoint creates an inset. But sometimes a fabric's lovely details get eliminated when an elaborate motif is jammed into a narrow point. Try shaping the template to the print. You might create a shape that's easier to sew and a design that reads like a point or is even better. Sharp points destined to rendezvous along the side seams are rendered best in allover prints.

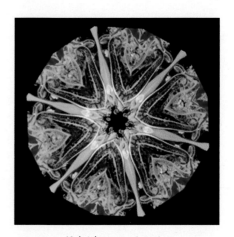

Kaleidoscope interior
by Knapp Studio.

ON-GRAIN VS. IN-A-GIRDLE

MY CONCEPT. Quilting textbooks advise you to cut patches on-grain. But when you're hunting and gathering for a kaleidoscope and fix your sight on a slanting stripe or a wandering paisley, the bottom line is you can't always play by those rules. Catch the motif, let the grain go. The exceptions are Patch 1 and the designated outer border of the quilt. As long as Patch 1 is cut on-grain and stability is provided by the final boundary, you can discipline interior off-grain patches to behave.

APPLYING THE CONCEPT. Stay stitching is one way to add stability to off-grain edges (so I've been told). But an idea I like even better is to girdle a block or a quilt with on-grain strips that exert firm control. The girdle solution raises a color question: whether to continue the already established hues and blur the transition so the girdle isn't noticeable, or whether to choose a contrasting color so the girdle functions like a frame.

Of course, any block that's headed into a traditional quilt setting is going to bump into sashing, which, when cut on-grain, will stabilize any unruly block behavior.

FAUX CURVES

MY CONCEPT. A line is a series of points. One day, my perspective on this fact reversed and led me to a brand-new skill. Instead of connecting points to make a line, I could draw any curved line, break it up into points an inch or less apart, and connect the dots from point to point with straight sew-able lines. Now I can parse a curvaceous contour into a chain of straight lines or smooth an austere line into a gently rounded arc. All of the quilts in the gallery are composed of straight lines only.

APPLYING THE CONCEPT. This insight has three applications. For Option 1, place the sharp point of a compass on the apex (the top point) of a triangle drafted on graph paper and pivot the leg equipped with a pencil, marking one-eighth of a perfect circle on the wedge. I often place this kind of circular line to the left and right of the center axis, not on it. This position means you need to make a mirror image template for the patch. Trace this curved line onto the see-through template with black permanent marker. Use this template to audition fabric motifs that mimic the line. When all of the wedges are sewn together, the result will appear to be as complete and accurate a circle as the compass-drawn one.

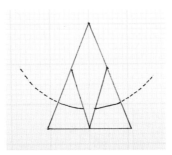

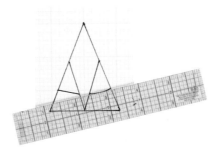

Option 2. Curves are drafted as straight seams.

Option 1. The curve is in the printed fabric.

Option 2 reforms curvy lines into straight ones using a ruler. Typically, I strip an allover fabric that contrasts highly with the seam it shares to make the circle shape obvious.

Option 3 begins by drawing a curved line on the graph paper diagram with a pencil. Sometimes I sketch freehand, sometimes I use a compass to draw a true circle, and sometimes I create the effect by accident. Align the straight edge of a short, narrow ruler with the curve, trying to position as long a stretch of the ruler as possible with the arc. Zip a pencil line along the ruler. Make sure the lines start and end at points of intersection on the graph paper grid; measurements are more reliable when the line travels from grid point to grid point. It depends on the arc of a curve, but with a true circle, about one inch agrees with the ruler at a time. Sometimes, rather than a single line, it takes a series to reform a curve.

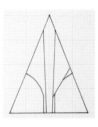

Option 3. A series of seams simulates a curve.

Any curve can be pieced this way. The key is: don't rely on the inaccurate eyeball method to straighten it out or approximate the alignment between neighboring patches. Make sure adjacent templates match.

Interrupting the curve

These straight-pretending-to-be-circular lines don't have to be continuous. We've already established that mirror images placed next to each other double the amount of pattern, sometimes forming a boring chunk. Revealing segments of a circle is more effective, suggesting that other fragments are temporarily in front of the circle, since the image is fleeting and bound to change in another second. The eye enjoys connecting them into a pleasing loop even when it skips-stops.

THE KALEIDOSCOPE LEGACY

MY CONCEPT. For over ten years, the state-of-the-art kaleidoscope has been both my design inspiration and my classroom. Analyzing what a scope is and also what it isn't has steered me in lots of valuable directions. Becoming a kaleidoscope aficionado has made me more adaptable and flexible. The notion that there is no best, absolute, correct fabric selection—that fabric choices made today will be different from ones made tomorrow—is very liberating. After all, a breathtaking collision of color in a kaleidoscope is bound to maneuver itself into something different in the instant it takes me to hand the scope to you.

Surprise. Magic. Change. Chance. In order to conjure the kaleidoscope persona and apply it to my quilting, I've learned to trust in symmetry, rely on detail, and believe that the whole will always be greater than the sum of its parts. No matter what direction my future quilts take, this personal design vocabulary, gleaned through the eyepiece of a kaleidoscope, will take the journey with me.

APPLYING THE CONCEPT. The word "kaleidoscope" conjures up images brimming with elaborate details and interlaced patterns. One way to achieve animated, dramatic impact is to use textiles printed with complex patterns.

Since kaleidoscopes rely on the reflection of light rays from mirrors, the interior image always seems luminous. This incandescent view taught me to stockpile fabrics that seem to emit self-generated light because they will lend this light to the quilt top.

I've also learned that fabrics and colors don't have to match. Focus on matching seams, not colors. Perfectly matched colors can be boring, while shades of a color evoke the translucent nature of a scope interior. An unconventional combination of fabrics simulates the appealing and random nature of a kaleidoscope. If you want to stick to a color family, be flexible. If something catches your eye, try it. You might not like every result, but he opportunity to self-critique has its rewards.

As quilters, we've inherited the notion that lines must be straight and uniformly even, like lattice. But the interior of a kaleidoscope reveals the opposite: lines capable of infinite variety. Every chance you get, draft lines that get narrower or wider as they travel. Sew on a classic stripe at an angle or cut it so different proportions of its line show. Even a small shift will multiply into a significant difference. Irregularity implies transience.

Think kaleidoscopically. Come to the table with a willingness to revise. Share control rather than demand obedience from your subject. When the fabric wants to go that way instead of this, let it. Rearrange fabrics, colors, shapes, and lines into new patterns constantly.

MY FABRIC

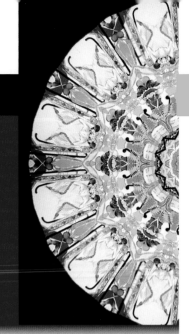

My approach to fabric excludes preconceived notions of what goes with what. Making a match between incongruent fabrics makes my day. Whether fabrics belong to different styles is not an issue for me. My agenda: to balance my sense of what a kaleidoscope looks like with my heartfelt belief that when it comes to fabric, more is MORE!

I need an eclectic mix of multitalented fabrics. Cloth is, after all, my palette, as valid as any other medium. I love fabrics that tickle my imagination: designs with hyper-abundant colors and charismatic patterns, prints that play well with both commercial and dyed stuff, textiles that sometimes set the stage and sometimes dance on it. I want it all, I want it now, and I make no excuses for the size of my stash. As I have often said, I feel sorry for the ones who don't get it.

The dictionary definition of "to match" is to be exactly alike. But using only stuff that is the exact same creates a flat, insipid effect, not the lively nuances that pop up when light and shadow play nicely together. Variety provides visual texture. My inclination is to balance glamour and usefulness. When possible, practice pieceful coexistence by placing a forgiving textile next to a fussy one. Consider the weight and fiber content of adjacent fibers. Good fabrics make good neighbors.

Over the years, I've developed a vocabulary to describe the personality and function of the fabrics I use. This personal lexicon divides fabrics into two categories: prima donnas and allovers.

DIRECTIONALITY

One way to classify patterned fabric is to acknowledge the directions they cause the eye to travel.

One Direction

A one-directional pattern is like a scene. Intuitively, it can only be viewed one way. For an example, see page 82.

Two Directions

An example of a two-directional print is a classic stripe, because the result is the same if it is flipped or turned 180°. For examples, see page 83.

Four Directions

The classic example of a four-directional print is a plaid, arranged in a box layout, which can be turned four ways. The term aptly describes the nameless genre of elaborate patterns I refer to as bilaterally symmetrical. For examples, see page 80.

PRIMA DONNAS

Prima donnas are powerful design elements. Simultaneously temperamental and charismatic, they are the divas that give a design its distinctive voice. Any fabric that is composed of motifs that are the exact duplicates of one another is a prima donna. Quilters call them "fussy cuts" because creating lots of identical patches requires effort. These high-maintenance fabrics need to be lavished with attention, but they always pay off. I rely heavily on intricately printed fabrics to render an image bursting with complexity.

Bilateral Symmetrical Fabric

The fussiest prima donnas are symmetrical, like a butterfly. Remember, this is the ideal fabric for Patch 1. A bilaterally symmetrical motif can be divided into identical or mirror-imaged halves by a line passing through the center. The layout is usually a mirror-repeat, from left to right, and sometimes from top to bottom, too.

Once you get to know them, symmetrical fabrics aren't very intimidating at all. Intricate designs arranged in ordered layouts are as invaluable as they are provocative. They challenge me to stretch and invent clever patchwork to maximize their graceful behaviors. The agile motifs soften the straight lines of the long seams, creating the illusion of graceful continuity. You'll grow to covet these clever and versatile illusion-makers because, in the end, you will get credit for the work that they do.

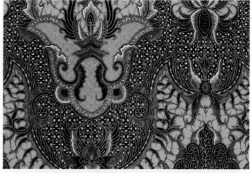

Bilateral symmetrical fabric yields many choices for Patch 1, such as the six options shown here.

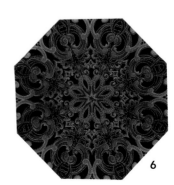

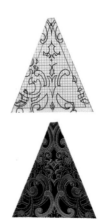

Pseudosymmetrical Fabric

Some motifs give the appearance of symmetry at first glance, but a closer inspection reveals differences between the two sides. I call these fabrics pseudosymmetricals. You want to be able recognize a symmetrical wannabe when you see one and learn what it can and cannot do.

You can use pseudosymmetrical patches to imitate symmetry as long as the patches don't touch one another. The eye will interpret the rhythmic repetition of elements as symmetrical even if the motifs are a little lopsided. Small discrepancies will not be noticed. Just don't position a motif lacking true bilateral symmetry where it is expected to match itself perfectly along both left and right seams simultaneously. If the two sides of the motif are different, they can't connect seamlessly to their mirror image, no matter how hard you try. And never push one of these into Patch 1. To detect an imposter, trace hints from the motif on template plastic. Flip the plastic over onto the assumed mirror image motif to see if the hints line up in exactly the same way.

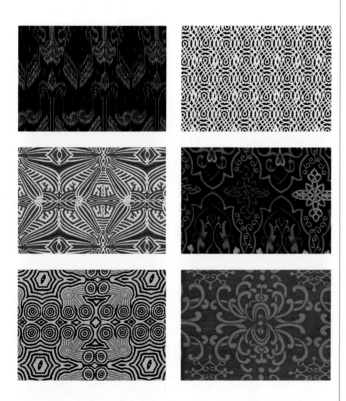

Where can you use pseudosymmetricals? Look for occasions where a patch isn't destined to meet itself coming and going. Place it along the center axis, but don't let the patch extend all the way from one side of the wedge to the other. Sometimes you can manipulate the junction between two quasi-symmetrical patches to neutralize the disparity. This solution depends on getting one set of the motif's edges to meet in an accurate mirror image along one edge of the patch. The rest of the motif will flow away from this joint in a slightly different way to the right than the left. No one will ever notice as long as the connecting seam between the two is clean and continuous. Treat the faux-symmetrical motif as if it's the real thing by using only one template, even though the hints on the template don't quite line up when it's reversed and flipped over.

A third option is to inject an **interruption**. If you don't want a patch to touch its nonidentical twin, break up the connection between them with something else, preferably an allover that can be stripped on. Patches destined to rendezvous along the side seams are rendered best in simple allover prints anyway. Then the assembly process doesn't demand matching both an intricate pattern and seam joints.

Mirror Image Motifs

Symmetrical fabrics aren't our only source of mirror image patches. Some fabrics contain individual mirror image motifs, such as butterflies, within a larger freestyle design. Another option is paired motifs, such as paisleys, but be careful; these can be deceptive. What seems to be a pair of mirror image figures, one wiggling left and the other wiggling right, often turns out to be one and the same figure rendered right-side-up and then upside-down, without actually being flipped over.

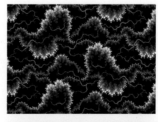

Classic Stripes

Stripes automatically slide the eye from here to there, forming visual pathways that instill an element of motion. One-way stripes have a distinct top and bottom and must be oriented in the same direction, but two-way stripes can be turned upside-down or right-side-up, and no one would notice. Either kind can be printed or woven.

I like to strip on skinny bands comprised of a multitude of colors. Realize that there's more than one way to strip a stripe. The effects are completely different if you cut parallel or perpendicular (or even diagonal) to the selvage, so audition which way you want the stripe positioned in the patch. Sketching the options on my graph paper diagram helps me decide.

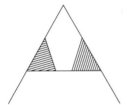

Stripes can go either way.

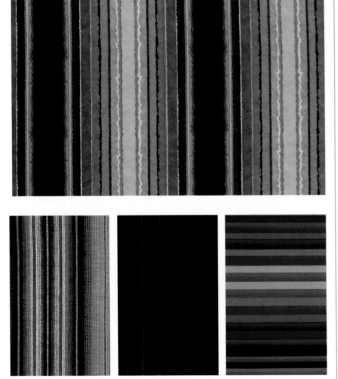

Wacky Stripes

I want you to expand your definition of stripes right now. Add function to your definition of this form. We're going to include any linear textile pattern that is capable of steering visual traffic, no matter how wide, wiggly, or irregular the bands.

Wacky stripes, as I call them, do have certain limitations. Zigzags and serpentine stripes infuse a lively quality, but their erratic behavior sometimes makes it difficult to create the illusion of a continuous line from patch to patch, especially in fairly small patches. Depending on the degree of color contrast, a herringbone or chevron provides a bouncing visual journey up and down the hills and valleys of its zigzag.

Hand-dyed panel, 44″ × 44″, from Lunn Studios.

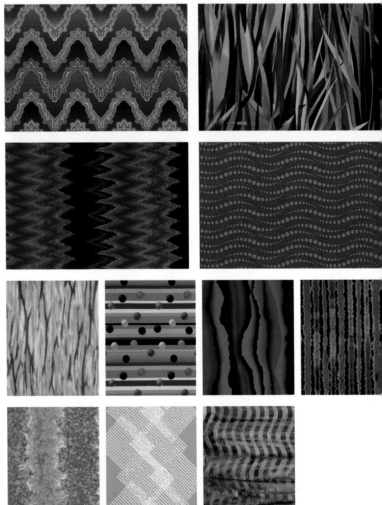

Ombré

Ombré is the textile designer's term for colors that gradually shade and blend into another. This adept transition from light to dark adds complexity while carrying the viewer's eye smoothly from one form to the next. Attaching a shadow to a basic stripe sets off vibrations that pop the stripe off a fabric's flat surface.

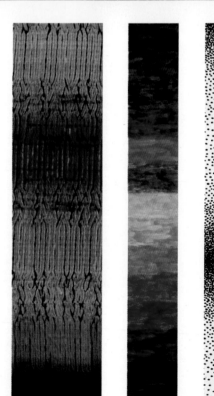

Symbiotic Fabric

Some fabrics don't look like much on their own, but when attached to other fabrics, they add pizzazz. There's a surprising mutual benefit to the relationship. One fabric accessorizes the other one. Sometimes just a snippet of the unassuming fabric helps you achieve an elegant, seamless outcome.

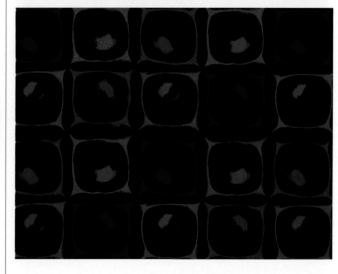

ALLOVERS

Allovers play a vital supporting role. Compared to the fussy prima donna, they are versatile and noncomplaining. The nondirectional design of the allover looks the same from any angle. There is no implicit top, bottom, left, or right. Its forgiving temperament makes it the fabric of choice to take on a strip-piecing adventure. I've identified several categories of allovers to suit my piecing needs.

Reads Like a Solid

For the record, I never use true solids. I hunt eternally for specimens crammed with an abundance of shading. These "read-like-a-solid" fabrics often become my source of luminosity. A finished product that seems dimensional is always more interesting.

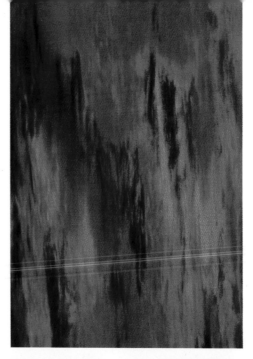

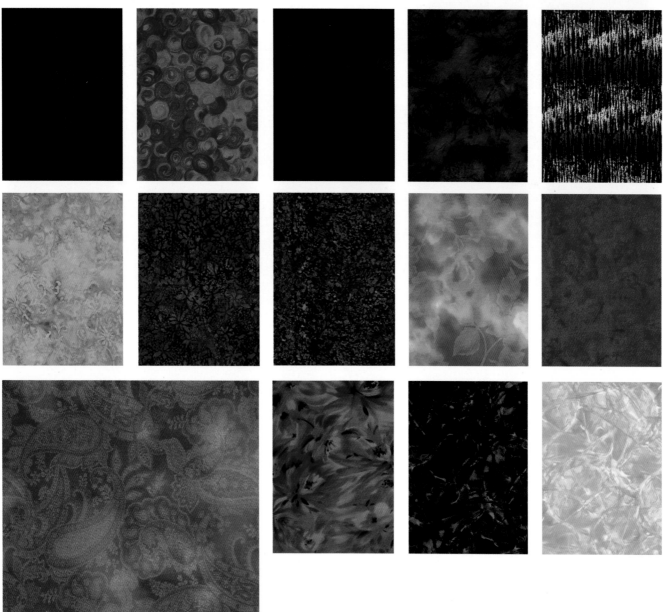

Prints

Prints with a multitude of internal colors are extremely valuable, as long as they can be stripped on randomly. Use them to blur a straight line, extend a neighboring patch, or turn a stiff, flat motif into a shimmering one. Here's the litmus test to see if a print can be used this way: fold it on top of itself so an arbitrary portion butts up against any other part of the print. If the fold seems to disappear and the print appears continuous, use it. This would not happen to a directional fabric folded in this manner.

Dots and Dashes

Fabrics printed with lots of colors in a tiny area energize the most disheartened design. Think dots. I like when dots go bonkers, splattering into colored patterns of randomly tossed speckles, like confetti. Dots organized in a sequential pattern cause the viewer's eye to play connect-the-dots, sparking a dynamic quality. Make the dots a little longer, and you've got dashes.

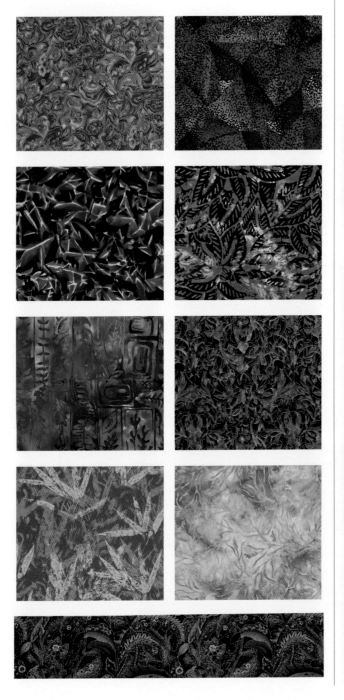

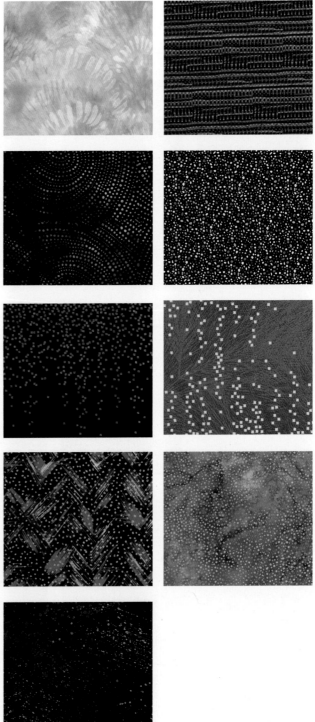

CLEVER FABRIC TRICKS

The Two-Faced Batik

Part of a batik's appeal is its relaxed, handmade look. Clearly, we would not expect reliable mirror images from these exotic, primitive motifs. Surprise! Batiks are reversible! Because of the dye process, the figures are often equally legible on both sides of the fabric. Usually, you can't tell the right from the wrong side; slight color shifts between the designated front and back can usually be ignored. If you've got curlicues whorling left, turn the fabric over and they'll be revolving to the right.

The Not-So-Sensuous Silk

The luminous colors of pure silk are simply irresistible. I know it sounds wicked, but I turn silk fabrics from slippery into stable by pressing fusible woven interfacing onto the back. Once the silk is relieved of its free-flowing drape, it strips and pieces just like a crisp cotton. Search in fabric shops geared to apparel makers for the most featherweight fusible available. (See Sources, page 125.) If you hand quilt, test how the interfacing needles. Some fusible adhesives strip the thread or impede the needle's piercing action.

Silk lined with fusible woven interfacing handles like cotton.

The Versatile Stripe

Think of a striped layout as bands of color stripped together. In a patch intended to be two pieced-together fabrics, substitute a stripe to create the effect of a narrow strip without a bulky seam. Just mark a line on the template where you'd like the stripe to fall, then position the template on the striped fabric. The line imitates a seamline, but in this case, it represents the demarcation between two color bands. Use the template to cut out eight patches in each direction. You can use this technique to work in conspicuous jabs of color, soft mellow lines, or even subtle curves.

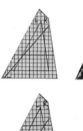

The Artistic License

When it comes to making a quilt, letting go of traditional practices—meaning, the way pioneer women did it—isn't cheating. It's innovative. You've got an overpowering element staring you in the face? Muffle it with an appliqué or embroider a few stitches or add a few beads to create a more graceful transition. Promise me you'll never call it cheating when you use a permanent marker to conceal some leftover particles of pattern that refused to get buried in the seam. Or let's say you find the perfect motif, but because the shape it's got to fit into is a tad too big, extraneous stuff piggybacks on it, tainting the view. Doesn't it seem clever to color over these misguided discrepancies? Go ahead. You're the designer. The block is yours. Who are you misleading? The aforementioned pre-industrial foremothers? Do you really think those make-do women would begrudge you a few clever, newfangled fixes?

the
TECHNICAL KALEIDOSCOPE

In 2003, when I exhibited in Japan, the place I wanted to visit more than any other was the Itchiku Kubota Kimono Museum, to see its namesake's masterful collection of kimonos created in the *Tsujigahana* method of tie-dye. On my first day in Japan, with jet lag nipping at my brain stem, I got myself there via public transportation. Exhausted and awe struck, I sat transfixed by a video of the elaborate process when I heard Kubota-san's dubbed-in voice saying in English, "I'm so short-tempered. Why did I think this up?"

That's exactly how I feel! Not that I'm short-tempered but I am kind of casual, if not sloppy, and I'm definitely not a technician. How interesting that my quilts end up seamed from many thousands of pieces, since I don't think there is inherent value in teensy slivers of fabric and perfect points. However, while I don't embrace technical achievement as a personal goal, I also don't want technical boo-boos to detract from the visual impact. In this chapter, I present the uncommon techniques that evolved to compensate for my less than stellar skills.

My Tools

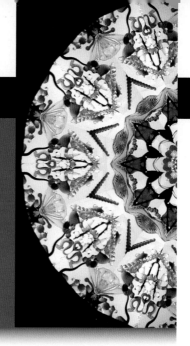

The truth is, I don't really sew very well, but I want it to look like I do. Fabricating this illusion means using reliable tools. Think of it as trying to start a fire by rubbing two sticks together. It becomes a whole lot easier if one of the sticks is a match. Using the same tools consistently from the beginning of a project to the end is just plain common sense. So is making sure all of your measuring devices (rulers, graph paper, template plastic) agree with one other. Otherwise, your carefully measured pieces might not fit together.

GRAPH PAPER. Choose an eight-to-the-inch grid and bold inch lines. The bold inch line makes the grid easier to read and allows you to use the graph paper as a ruler. I buy Bienfang graph paper in 11″ × 17″ and 17″ × 22″ pads.

SEE-THROUGH GRIDDED TEMPLATE PLASTIC. Once again, choose an eight-to-the-inch grid and bold inch lines. You usually get four 8½″ × 10¾″ sheets in a package. I find 12″ × 18″ sheets very awkward. Do not purchase long sheets rolled and sold in a tube. You could flatten these under your mattress for a year, and they'll curl right back into a roll as soon as they make their escape.

C-THRU RULERS. The C-Thru Ruler company makes thin, clear, see-through plastic rulers marked with a ⅛″ grid. I keep a 6″ × 1″ ruler next to me, a 12″ × 2″ close by, and an 18″ × 2″ within hailing distance. Thicker rulers made for use with rotary cutters cast shadows and don't allow a pen or pencil to get really, really close to the ruler's edge. See page 95 for a tip on why I use the C-Thru brand exclusively for adding seam allowance to templates. It's worth reading.

PENCILS.

PENCIL SHARPENER. A sharpener is a must to keep lead pencil tips pointy. Lines don't only have length. They also have width. When you outline a shape, you increase its size by the width of the marked pencil line.

ERASERS.

COMPASS. The child's school version is all you need.

SILVER-COLORED GEL INK PENS. You need a way to mark thin, permanent, visible cutting lines (not sewing lines) on dark-colored fabrics. I used to use white chalk pencils, which required constant sharpening. Then I discovered those newfangled, light-colored, acid-free permanent gel ink pens. Silver is the best color with the potential for glaring visibility. My favorite pen is the Sanford Uniball Gel Impact 1.0mm.

Okay, I know what you're thinking: What if gel inks turn out to be hole-causing time bombs? Here's my justification: a gel pen doesn't bleed, and since you cut fabric patches by aiming straight down the middle of the marked line, most of the line disappears anyway. Should anything go chemically amiss a hundred years from now, there's barely any residue to wreak havoc, and it's all located in the seam allowance anyhow. In the meantime, you're able to see the line, enjoy the process, feel successful, and keep blood pressure down. What could be bad?

EXTRA FINE-POINT BLACK PERMANENT MARKERS. A marker should leave a thin yet visible line on template plastic and glide smoothly without stretching the fabric. I don't want a plump line increasing the size of my template or patch, and I don't want to waste time searching for a line once it's drawn. For this task, I use a Pilot extra-fine-point black permanent type marker SCA-UF.

FABRIC SCISSORS AND TEMPLATE/PAPER SCISSORS. Get two first-rate scissors that fit your hand and hide them from the rest of your family when you're not using them. Personally, I like six- to eight-inch serrated blades. A template scissors should not be

the discarded kitchen shears or shaped for a five-year-old's hand. It is *the* essential, indispensable tool from which all other acts follow. I use Olfa SCS-1 multipurpose scissors.

ROTARY CUTTER, RULER, AND SELF-HEALING CUTTING MAT. For trimming patches, I use the Brooklyn Revolver, which is a circular rotary mat mounted on a lazy Susan (see Sources, page 125), and a small 30mm rotary cutter.

FINE PINS. I like silk pins or Clover glass-headed extra-fine pins (.40 × 36mm), which smoothly pass through fabrics. Make sure the package says .40 and Fine.

SEWING MACHINE. The machine must have a well-defined ¼″ seam allowance guide. Use a single-hole, or straight stitch, throat plate to promote perfect stitch quality and to prevent distortion and jamming that occurs when the fabric is pulled into larger holes. A single hole facilitates the piecing of small patches, especially at the beginning and end of seams.

GOOD LIGHTING. Without it, anticipate eyestrain and frustration, courtesy of a palette filled with dark fabrics.

MIRRORS (OPTIONAL). Two mirrors, hinged or held together at the correct angle and placed on top of a fabric, can become a design tool for identifying the results when mirror-imaged motifs multiply.

A DESIGN WALL (OPTIONAL). This flat, vertical surface lets you view and evaluate your quilt-in-process. To convert an available wall into a design wall, line it with batting or plain flannel fabric to hold patches in place without pinning.

How to Draft an Angle

Please. Trust me on this one. Drafting an accurate angle is not about math. It's about learning a new, intuitive behavior. I promise that if you (1) follow me through the next three pages, (2) have the correct supplies, and (3) don't panic when you see a chart, you will not only make a near-perfect angle, you won't even notice the learning curve.

First of all, let's establish why it is so important to draft a reliable angle.

A kaleidoscope is basically a circular design composed of identical triangular wedges that radiate from a center point. When joined together, the wedges, no matter how many there are, equal 360°. (For the record, this is practically all the math I know, and now you know it too.) This geometric tidbit is the key that enables identical slices of patchwork pie to fit together properly. The size, the design, the intricacy, the colors, and the very fabric of the kaleidoscope are subjective and up to you, but the fact of the matter is that all of the wedges add up to 360°. This fact cannot be ignored, modified, or adjusted.

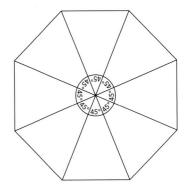

Kaleidoscope block created from eight 45° triangles.

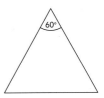

60° triangle

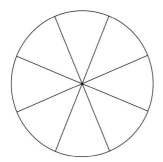 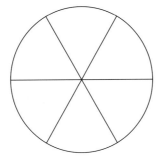

Triangular-shaped wedges radiate from the centers of two circles.

Decide how many wedges you'd like your design to be made up of. Six or eight is typical (I use eight for the examples in this book). On rare occasions, you might go for ten. Next, calculate the angle of the triangle by dividing 360° by the number of wedges. For example, 360° divided by 8 wedges equals 45° per wedge.

45° triangle

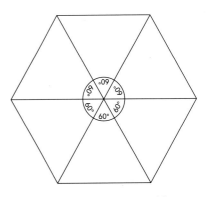

Kaleidoscope block created from six 60° triangles.

That's the theory. But what if, instead of 45°, you err on the generous side and one extra seemingly insignificant degree slips into the tip of your triangle? Now, instead of 45°, you are multiplying 46° by 8, which equals 368°. Those extra 8° have to go somewhere and, rather than the intended flat center, a nipple will erupt. Sadly, this is not one of those situations you can press your way out of. Skimp on a measly degree (44° × 8 = 352°), and the center collapses into an unsightly crater. In either case, you'll feel the overwhelming urge to appliqué something over the design's crucial center.

One more bit of geometry and we're there. It turns out a triangle is not only 45° at its tip. The two sides, whether they measure 5″ or 105″, must also maintain an accurate 45° angle along their entire length. If they don't, the block won't lie flat when all eight triangles are sewn together. The same 360° needed in the center for a graceful start is needed at the outer edges for a grand Esther Williams style finale. Too many degrees and the perimeter wiggles where you were expecting nice and flat. Less than 360° and a ball starts to form.

There's no getting around it. The angle you draft has got to be pretty perfect. It becomes the archetype, the original model from which all your other triangles will be derived. Whatever is done to the design once will be repeated six or eight or ten times. Every success, and every mistake, will be multiplied by the number of pieces of pie.

Graph paper with a ⅛″ grid is crucial for drafting an accurate triangle. Start by locating a bold vertical line running down the middle of the page. Think of it as the backbone of your triangle or the belly of a butterfly. Ultimately, any fabric pattern or combination of patches visible to the left of this line will appear equidistant to the right of the line in a mirror image. I designate this line the center axis; in geometric circles, it is called the axis of reflection or line of symmetry. In the following diagrams, the center axis appears as a dotted line for easy identification. *Do not mark the center axis on your graph paper.* Only mark sewing lines inside the graph paper triangle. If you mark the center axis, you risk interpreting it as a sewing line later on.

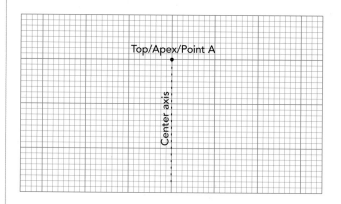

Note that the top of the center axis, point A, is the tip, a.k.a. the apex, of the triangle. It's really important to situate point A at the intersection of the center axis and a bold horizontal line rather than arbitrarily at one of the ⅛″ lines in between. This allows you to use the graph paper like a ruler, a technique you will learn to rely on and appreciate.

PLOTTING POINTS TO DRAFT A 45° ANGLE

Vertical	Horizontal
1½″	⅝″
3⅝″	1½″
5⅛″	2⅛″
7¼″	3″
8¾″	3⅝″
12⅜″	5⅛″
16″	6⅝″
17½″	7¼″
21⅛″	8¾″
24¾″	10¼″

Vertical = length along center axis
Horizontal = left and right distance from center axis

If you plotted point A at the junction of two bold lines, the next part is easy. To use the chart, locate the first entry in the Vertical column (1½″). Beginning at point A, count down 1½″ along the center axis. Resist the urge to mark a pencil dot. Instead, position a ruler horizontally on the 1½″ grid line. Read across the chart to find the corresponding number in the Horizontal column (⅝″). Starting from the center axis, and with the ruler still firmly planted on the 1½″ horizontal line, count off ⅝″ to the left and make a visible but minuscule mark (point L). Go back to the center axis and repeat to the right (point R).

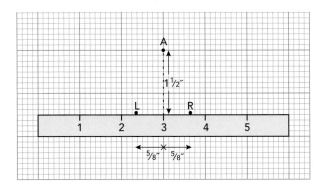

Plotting the first set of points.

Continue by moving the ruler down to the chart's next Vertical measurement (3⅝″), read across the chart, and plot the corresponding left and right points (1½″).

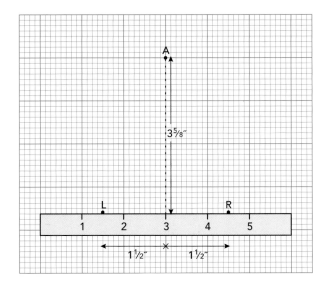

Plotting the second set of points.

Repeat the process until you have marked three or more left and right dot positions. Connect the dots to the apex with a straight line and you will have an accurate 45° wedge.

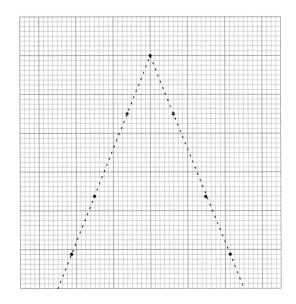

Once again, the reason why I don't mark the vertical length measurements on the graph paper is to keep the interior of the triangle as clear as possible. Once we finish drafting the angle and move onto the design stage, markings made to draft the angle become confusing artifacts. We have new marks to make, new fabrics to measure. This requires a triangular *tabula rasa*, waiting spotless and pristine.

See the Appendix for the Kaleidoscope Quilt Triangle Measurements Chart, page 122, divined through the magic of computers and the skills of Sue Helzer of College Park, Maryland, and Susan Feldman of Kirkwood, Missouri. It will enable you to draft a multitude of angles up to 25″ long. This means you now have the skills to make a fifty-inch-long kaleido-scope block, and that is a very cool fact.

TEMPLATING

Since I believe in giving credit where credit is due, I want to thank my long-time collaborator, the See-Through Template, for leading me places I would never have gone on my own. Without it, I'm just your everyday quilter. Put a template in my hand and I have super powers. Not only can I leap tall piles of fabric in a single bound, I can also contort myself like a rubbery super hero and explore fabric from every possible angle, without leaving my seat.

If you think of templates as the T-word, get over it. In recent years, templates have gotten a bad rap, perhaps because they've been outlawed from the lexicon of quick and easy quilts. There is a time and a place for templates, and that time is now. Using transparent template material and marking the seam allowance on it creates a template that functions like a window. This frame allows you to identify the area of the fabric that will be visible in the patch.

When I first set eyes on an intricately patterned fabric, I see the whole design laid out the way it was styled, typically in a top-to-bottom, left-to-right orientation. With the second glance, my mind's eye gets to work, skipping about, exploring, trying to isolate fragments of the pattern and predict which ones might morph into something spectacular when joined with other fabrics in the wedge *du jour.*

I'm not only looking for distinctive motifs to center in the patch. My focus is simultaneously aimed toward the seamline. Why care about what lands at the seamline? Because kaleidoscopically speaking, the motif that winds up along the seamline connects to its mirror image or joins forces with a motif in the adjacent patch. If the goal is to cause a motif to float elegantly against the kaleidoscope's common background, the search is on for a fabric with a background color similar to the one in your hand. Each of these cases results in a camouflaged connection. Seamlines will disappear, intricacy will reign, and you will get credit for the magic that happens (even when you are just as surprised by the results as everyone else).

Sounding clairvoyant about how a motif might behave means *bubkes.* Figuring out how to shape a template for that motif, transfer its measurements to graph paper, and create an exact replica multiple times—now *that* is an impressive feat. That's the job of a transparent template—and my next subject for dissection.

HOW TO MAKE A TEMPLATE

No matter how complex a shape is, the technique for making a template is always the same. Let's say we want to make a template for Patch 2 of the graph paper diagram.

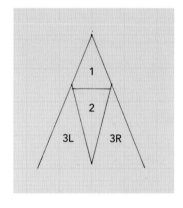

Lay a sheet of template plastic on the diagram over Patch 2, leaving enough template material to add a ¼″ seam allowance all around. When the patch straddles the center axis (as Patch 2 does here), *always* align a bold inch line of the template grid on the center axis, even if this means using a new sheet of template plastic. Carefully align the squares of the template material to the squares of the graph paper. If the margin around the grid on the template plastic is $\frac{1}{4}''$ or wider, use the margin as one of the seam allowances. Trace the patch outline onto the template plastic using a ruler and permanent pen. This outline indicates the sewing lines. Make sure the lines are dark and legible, slim but not fat. Anemic lines are ineffectual markers. Chunky ones are misleading.

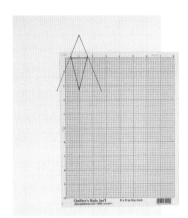

Trace the patch outline.

Next, add the seam allowance. On an eight-to-the-inch grid ruler, each square is $\frac{1}{8}''$ and two squares equal $\frac{1}{4}''$. Align the ruler's $\frac{1}{4}''$ delineation on the edge of the patch so that $\frac{1}{4}''$ extends beyond the patch and the rest of the ruler rests on it.

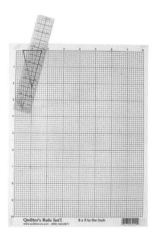

Add a $\frac{1}{4}''$ seam allowance.

Zip a line with the thin permanent marker along the ruler edge. Do this along every edge of the template. To avoid smearing (or schmearing, as we say in the Bronx), wait a beat before removing the ruler to give the ink a chance to dry. If smears and blotches do occur, don't panic. They are annoying but not fatal.

Cut out the template, aiming down the center of the marked line. I use scissors. Use a rotary cutter or precision utility knife if either is your cutting gadget of choice. The objective is to maintain, not increase or decrease, a template that will be used to cut identical patches. Each template should be the Platonic example of itself.

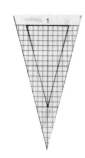

Cut out the template.

When adding seam allowance to an extremely acute angle, provide lots of space on the template plastic for the elongated pointy seam allowance that results.

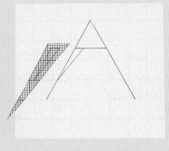

On some eight-to-the-inch grid rulers, the measure along one edge is slightly narrower than $\frac{1}{8}''$ by a miniscule, barely visible amount. This variance—whether deliberate or accidental—compensates for the width of a permanent marker line drawn along it. To determine which edge is the top, hold the ruler so the manufacturer's logo is at the bottom. Usually, the opposite edge is the top, narrower edge, although sometimes it is the bottom edge. Tag this narrower side with permanently marked arrows and use it consistently. If this sounds like the ranting of an overly fastidious technocrat, consider what's in store for one single triangular wedge composed of a mere ten patches, each with three sides. If an extra line width is added along with each seam allowance, the wedge plumps up by an additional thirty widths. Multiply this surplus by eight wedges and now picture 180 extra line widths, joining forces, spreading out, wreaking havoc. Anal retentive? No, just common sense. I use the C-Thru brand of rulers exclusively for adding seam allowance to templates.

TWO TYPES OF TEMPLATES

Symmetrical

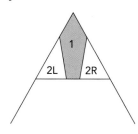

A symmetrical template is a template that can be divided into identical halves by a line passing through its center. It is reversible, reading the same from left to right or right to left. Any patch centered on the axis, such as Patch 1, is both symmetrical and reversible. Always use template plastic with a grid and bold inch lines to make symmetrical templates. Align a bold line of the grid directly on the midline of the patch. This simple strategy supports accuracy. Marking the shape on the template plastic at random, without regard for the bold lines, cancels out the grid's purpose and will, in fact, confuse you when you're caught up in the design process.

Mirror Image

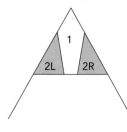

Templates for mirror image patches require special attention. Here, patches 2L and 2R are the mirror image of one another. Each shape is non-reversible and asymmetrical. Note that the pair sits equidistant, left and right of the center axis. To obtain an accurate mirror image of such a shape, you need to make only one see-through template. Use it first to mark eight 2L patches, then flip it over and use it wrong side up to mark eight 2R patches. Sharing the same template is more accurate than making two templates for each pair of mirror image patches.

Marking directional cues on asymmetrical templates is crucial. With many shapes, you'll find the correct orientation is not immediately obvious once the template is cut out. Without some sort of reminder, you risk placing a template topsy-turvy on the carefully selected fabric motif or cutting all sixteen patches in one direction.

Here's my reference system. To orient the template to the graph paper diagram, I immediately mark "L" and "R" at the top of every template within the margins of the seam allowance. I complete this step as soon as I've traced the template, before removing the template from the fabric, and before adding seam allowance. When I pick up the template (the next day or the next decade), I automatically know which end is up because the cues are toward the top.

The system works because I consistently make templates for patches on the left side of the wedge only. Every template is correctly aligned to the left side and must be flipped over and used wrong side up to cut the mirror image patch for the right side. When the letters are legible, I know the template is aligned to the left side. When the template is flipped over and the letters are reversed, I know the template is aligned to the right side. Make marking the directional cues L and R part of your template-making routine, as habitual as adding seam allowance.

Since asymmetrical patches are not positioned along the center axis, it is not necessary to align the bold lines of the grid any particular way. Let the guiding principle for placement—thou shalt not waste template plastic—be your positioning guide.

To conserve fabric, position a mirror image template to the right and left of the belly or center axis, not directly on it. Suppose you need eight 2L and eight 2R. If the Template 2 touches down on the center, you will need 16 prima donna motifs to cut all the patches. If you place the template a bit to the left and right of the center axis, you will need only eight motifs.

HOW TO MARK A TEMPLATE

Once you've decided where to position the template on the fabric, hold it in place and use the fine-point, black, permanent marker to trace a lot of the details of the selected motif directly onto the template. These marks will ensure perfect alignment and help you find identical patches multiple times. Let's synchronize our vocabulary and agree to call these traced markings *clues* rather than *registration marks*. Although the intent is the same, the means to the goal is the opposite. Registration marks are minute, inconspicuous marks positioned in an unobtrusive way. But once you remove the template from a complexly patterned fabric, shy and subtle marks won't guide you back to the original position.

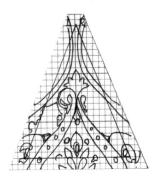

Forget about self-effacing. We want lots of in-your-face clues, obvious and distinctive eye-catching clues, the conspicuous kind that will identify the position quickly and accurately. If the motif has an outline composed of two lines, as many intricate designs do, trace both lines. Otherwise, you don't know which line you should use to anchor your design when you're marking the fabric. Attach a name to a motif while you're tracing it so this label gets fixed in your memory, making it easier to find: "Where are those noxious nail clippings?" "Where are those ruby red Betty Boop lips?" "Where's that gaggle of gilded curlicues?"

It's very important to let some of your markings spill across the seamlines into the seam allowance. This step facilitates accuracy at the seams, where the actual matching and sewing takes place.

MATCHING TEMPLATES

In traditional patchwork, when you stitch a square to a square or a half-square triangle to another half-square triangle, the angles along the edges being joined are the same. In kaleidoscopic patchwork, more often than not, you have to piece one irregularly shaped patch to another along a common seam. You try, reasonably, to place Patch 2 against Patch 3.

Uh-oh, there's a problem. The conventional technique learned in patchwork—match the edges and corners and then stitch—doesn't work. The angles are different, and they don't line up.

What you really want to align are the sewing points, ¼″ in from the cut edges, but how do you do it without guidelines to properly position the patches of fabric together? The sharper the angles to be pieced, the more difficult it is to eyeball the correct alignment. We can never assume the corner angles of neighboring templates are identical or that they match "close enough." Templates either match each other or they don't. Estimating is not a viable option. We need foolproof. We don't care what the angles are. We just want them to fit together as effortlessly as a Nine-Patch.

Solution 1: Trimming One Template to Another Template

Use this method when you have two templates to align.

1. Make the two templates as usual.

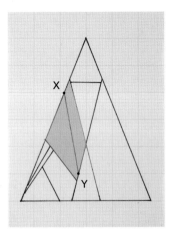

Before trimming.

2. Place the templates right sides together, as if they were fabric patches you were sewing together. Align the sewing lines and match points X and Y. Now look closely at the template plastic in the vicinity of each point X. See how a little fragment of extra plastic sticks out beyond the edge? Like the turned down corner of a page in a book, I call tidbits of template that peek past a significant other *dog ears*.

3. Using the rigid edge of the top template as a guide, mark and trim off the excess dog ear on the template underneath.

4. Repeat Steps 2 and 3, this time addressing the area around point Y. (You may need to turn the matched templates over.) This finishing step is important. It's not enough to know where to start sewing. The end of the sewing line must also correspond. An accurate match extends from cut edge to cut edge. Otherwise, when you are sitting at the machine, aligning the patches and sewing, you won't know what to aim for and can end up stretching a patch too much or not enough.

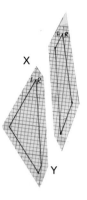

After trimming.

Solution 2: Devising a New Angle

Sometimes the difference between the two corners of neighboring templates is a minuscule sliver of plastic. Trimming off this dinky excess will not produce an edge-to-edge match you can really count on. Such a small amount can easily be overlooked or misunderstood, seen more as a faulty scissor snip than a deliberate alteration. In situations where there isn't an obvious dog ear, you should make one.

1. Make the templates as usual.

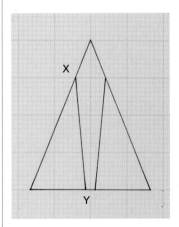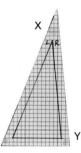

2. Check the match. Trim the dog ears at point X. Note the lower corner needs more definition for a more accurate match.

3. Invent a new blunt angle on either template, preserving approximately ¼″ seam allowance. Mark and cut.

4. Realign the templates and trim as described in Solution 1, page 98. When this operation is complete, the two corners will clearly match.

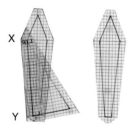

Solution 3: Trimming the Template to the Diagram

Solutions 1 and 2 assume you have access to both neighboring templates. But sometimes, before you can design an adjoining shape, you need to cut patches from a template with an overabundance of seam allowance stored in its corners. Common sense urges you to trim the surplus before you waste all that yummy fabric.

Stop! If you trim it without coordinating it to its neighbor, you risk shortchanging the amount of seam allowance needed. The result might be an impossible-to-compensate-for gap in the final seam, even if you deliberately leave a generous amount. Chances are you will clip it at a sensible angle, parallel to the template grid, while the required slant is more wacky and impossible to predict. Here's how to avoid a shortfall.

1. Make the template as usual.

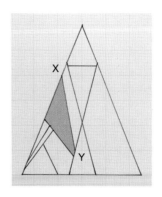

2. Position the template face up on its corresponding shape on the graph paper diagram. Flip the template over onto the diagram, right sides together, aligning the template's marked sewing line to the line representing the seam on the diagram.

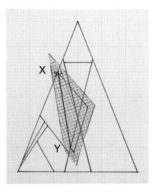

Graph diagram with template right sides together.

Now, if the diagram seamline had a ¼″ seam allowance added to it—the way templates do—you would be able to use the edge of the seam allowance to trim away any dog ears from the template. So, with a ruler, add the seam allowance line to the diagram in very light pencil, knowing that you want to erase it ASAP.

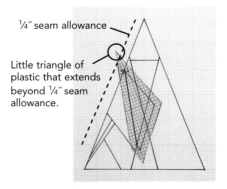

Same diagram with ¼″ seam allowance marked.

3. Realign the template face down on the diagram, as in Step 2. See the little triangle of plastic that extends beyond the penciled seam allowance? Using the penciled line as a guide, mark and trim off this protruding tip.

Trimmed template

4. Repeat for the bottom tip. Immediately erase the simulated seam allowance. Remember, only actual sewing lines are allowed on the diagram.

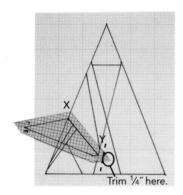

Same diagram with ¼″ seam allowance marked

You can now rely on both of the template's cropped edges to cut out patches primed for proficient piecing.

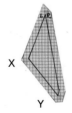

Trimmed template

How to Mark the Fabric

Place the template face up on the front side of the fabric, superimposing the clues on the template to the motifs on the fabric. Once the position is just right, trace around the edge of the template with a silver gel pen or black permanent pen, whichever will be more visible. To mark additional identical patches, align the template on the next available motif and repeat the process. Be sure your fabric has enough motifs for your scope; count before you cut.

Occasionally, a line you mark will be indistinguishable from a fabric's printed design lines. If this ever happens to you, turn the fabric over and see if the print is recognizable from the wrong side. If it is, you can try marking that side instead. (If you do end up marking an asymmetrical template on the wrong side of the fabric, be sure to flip the template over, too. Two wrongs make a right.)

If you haven't already experienced it, I'm sorry I have to be the one to warn you about an annoying fabric anomaly called *bowing*. After marking a bunch of identical patches that need to be fussy cut on a fabric with an obvious, regular repeat, you find that the next row of the repeat no longer lines up with the template. This problem is most noticeable in patterns with straight horizontal lines, such as printed plaids and border prints. It occurs when the fabric's warp and weft do not run perpendicular to each other. The tendency toward bowing begins in the greige (pronounced gray) goods stage, which refers to the raw base cloth that comes off a loom, before it is bleached, dried, and dyed for delivery to the end user. Once the fabric is printed, significant bowing cannot be remedied. To compensate, try moving the template to a row a comparable distance from the selvage. For example, if you are successful lining up the template ten inches from the selvage, try the row ten inches from the other selvage next.

HOW TO CUT THE FABRIC

Here's where your quilting persona determines the process. If you are a rotary-cutting connoisseur, go for it. You probably ignored "How to Mark the Fabric" anyway, since your plan is to place the template on the fabric and rotary cut around it.

I use scissors, cutting out the patch, aiming down the center of the marked line. The objective is to maintain, not increase or decrease, the size of the patch. Fussy-cutting lots of identical patches means you'll end up with a holey fabric. Do yourself a favor and don't show it to those nonquilters you live with. It's not to your advantage.

A scissors doesn't have to be long to cut a single patch of fabric. You want dexterity, not power. I like a 6″ scissors with sharp, serrated blades. As a devout lefty, I prefer ambidextrous scissors. Very few lefties learned to cut with left-handed scissors, which turns out not to be an intuitive skill picked up easily at an age when you can finally afford a good left-handed scissors. You just don't know which side of the blade to aim for.

THE PATCH 1 PERSONA

Patch 1's unique design duties are fraught with technical accountability. Since a radial design automatically draws the viewer's attention toward the center, the confluence of eight identical Patch 1s becomes the primary focal point. This pivotal position assumes a major role, seducing the viewer into the emotional center. To experience what I mean, the next time you're looking at a kaleidoscopic image, close your eyes and then open them. Your eye is drawn first into the center of the scope and only then begins traveling out among the interlaced patterns.

Patch 1 sprawls from one side of the triangle to the other. At the seams, the motifs meet, match, and reflect themselves into mirror images. Patch 1 reveals itself eight times in the center and bumps into itself along the left and right legs of each triangular wedge. It's an extremely high-profile spot demanding a fabric capable of delivering the illusion of graceful seamlessness. Only a pattern loaded with compulsive symmetry can pull it off, because if the motif along the left seam isn't an exact mirror image of the one on the right, their mismatched connection

implies they bashed haphazardly into each other because someone sewed badly. What I'm trying to say is, Patch 1 must be cut from a bilaterally symmetrical fabric, meaning a line drawn down the middle will divide the design into identical halves, like the wings on a butterfly.

In addition to its bilateral properties, a motif worthy of Patch 1 must be cut on a straight grain of fabric. After Patch 1, you can throw sewing caution to the wind and indulge your every off-grain whim. The on-grain alignment—center axis of the patch on the lengthwise or crosswise grain of the goods—promotes stability during the last step when all of the finished triangles are sewn together. When you want to rip and try again because the center is too mismatched for your taste, the stability provided by on-grain patches will let you try again and even again. I believe that even those who don't like symmetry expect precision in the center.

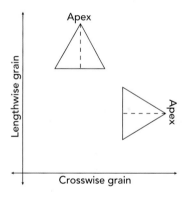

Always cut Patch 1 on-grain.

The final shape of Patch 1 depends on the particular motif you choose. The apex will, of course, be a 45° or 60° angle, but the remaining edges can be tailored to accommodate the motif. It doesn't have to be a horizontal line turning the shape into a triangle. Here are some possibilities:

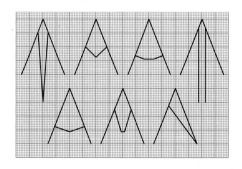

Options for the shape of the first patch

One more point (pun intended): see how the seam allowance at the tip extends into a point bigger than 1/4″? Imagine the impact when six, eight, or ten of these bulked-up angles meet in the middle. Don't just snip off the tip willy-nilly. Using a ruler, mark a seam allowance 1/4″ beyond the tip and then cut carefully through the middle of the marked line.

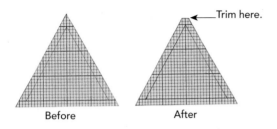

Before   After   Trim here.

THE PATCH 1/PATCH 2 INTERFACE

I wish I could be sitting next to you at the design table right now. It would be a lot easier for both of us if I could show you the following important procedure rather than put it into many, many, many words. But, trooper that I am, I'm going to pop a piece of chocolate in my mouth and soldier up to the task. Your assignment is to read it until you get it.

Choose the first and second patches together. If you pick Patch 1 without regard for Patch 2, you are wasting your time. Finding a transition after the patch is cut is harder than finding a link between them right from the start. The goal is to uncover a connection that will obscure the seam for an uninterrupted flow from one patch to the next, drawing the eye away from the center and out along new visual pathways. Finding such a relationship requires physically manipulating the fabric and asking lots of "what if" questions.

To get started, put the fabric intended for Patch 1 on your work surface. Next, look for tempting portions of another fabric that suggest a relationship with the first, perhaps because the backgrounds are comparably colored or a motif in Fabric 2 reminds you of something in Fabric 1. Investigating a possible link involves folding the second fabric along the place that caught your eye. The fold represents a potential seam. Place Fabric 2 on top of Fabric 1, positioning the crease where you envision the bottom edge of the first patch will be. Trust your eye. If the fold virtually disappears, so you can't tell where one

fabric ends and the other begins, you have a keeper. If your eye detects a line between 1 and 2, fine-tune the connection by adjusting the fold, a little deeper, a little less. Or, move Fabric 2 so it sits a little higher on Fabric 1, seeking to link a motif from one fabric directly into the other. Nope, move it down. More. Now turn Fabric 2 upside down and see if it reads better from that direction. If not, reach for another fabric and start auditioning again.

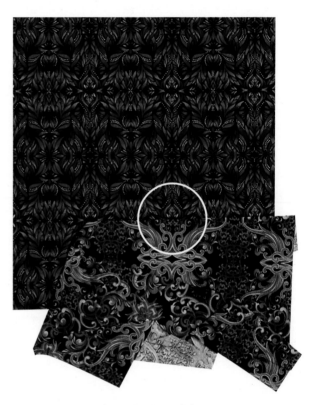

Investigating a link

I do it this way because I don't want to waste a repeat. Unless I have tons of it, I don't like to cut out prima donnas until I've decided on a patch's finished version. Stop when an appreciative "Ooooh!" slips out of your mouth. I call this the Ooooh Factor. Trust this involuntarily sighed sign of approval.

Have your sheet of template plastic—marked with the 45° angle—ready and handy to audition the possibilities. Remember, don't cut out the triangle and don't add seam allowance to it. You are now going to tailor templates 1 and 2 to fit the chosen motifs, not the other way around. Use the grid of the template as a ruler to measure the size and shape of the patches, making the necessary alterations before you do any cutting.

Place the entire sheet of template plastic on top of the two fabrics, aligning the marked triangle's bold center axis along the apparent center of the Patch 1 motif, what I refer to as "the belly of the butterfly."

Every time you reposition the sheet of template plastic and audition a new possibility, ask yourself:

- What lands along the center axis?

- What lands along the seamlines?

- What lands in the apex of the triangle?

- What happens if the template starts a little higher?

- Now what lands on the axis and along the seamlines?

Once you've found what you like, hold the template plastic in place, look through it, and locate the seamline between patches 1 and 2. Remember, it is easier to rely on a measurement if the line travels from grid point to grid point. Adjust the template as needed and then mark the line on the template. Next, trace hints of the motifs from both fabrics to the template using a permanent marker. Do this immediately, before things shift and this perfect spot is lost forever.

Mark the master template.

Using the template as a ruler, count down from the top of the triangle to measure the distance from the apex to the seamline between Patch 1 and Patch 2. In Kaleidoscope A, it's $1\frac{5}{8}''$. Transfer this measurement to the graph paper diagram by counting down $1\frac{5}{8}''$ from that triangle's apex. Using a pencil, draw the seamline on the graph paper diagram.

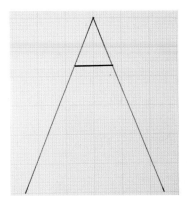

Transfer the seamline to the diagram.

Now you can focus on shaping Patch 2. Its bottom contour doesn't have to be a horizontal line from one side of the triangle to the other. Often the motif chosen to connect to Patch 1 joins smoothly with Patch 1's center design, but bears no relationship to the patterns on the left and right sides. It's often extraneous or boring or distracting or filled with asymmetrical motifs that can't mirror image. If you don't want 'em, whack 'em off.

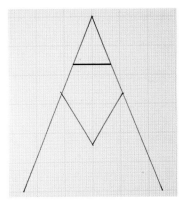

Shape the bottom contour of Patch 2.

Once you've designed, measured, and transferred Patch 2 to the diagram, your master template can be turned into either Template 1 or Template 2 but not both, because there's no way to accommodate two sets of seam allowances at their mutual junction.

I use short 6″ rulers to shape Patch 2. The idea is to frame the area you want to be visible in the patch. Position the rulers on top of the template and use straight edges to define potential shapes for the template. Remember to lay the rulers so the outlines they form start and end at points of intersection on the grid. Once you reach a decision, don't remove the rulers. Hold them firmly in place and draw lines along the straight edges to define Template 2. Transfer these lines to the graph paper diagram by counting off the grid lines.

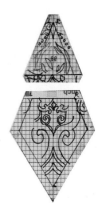

Make separate templates for
Patch 1 and Patch 2.

Shaping a patch using rulers.

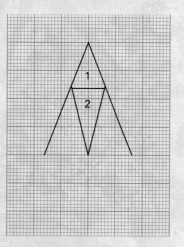

Mark the seamlines
on the diagram.

The cut out patches   A seamless
                          version of
                          Patch 1 & 2

If you decide to turn it into Template 1, your next step is to make a Template 2 with seam allowance, before cutting the master apart. How? Put another piece of template material on the master template and trace Template 2 using a ruler and a permanent marking pen. Add the seam allowance and cut out the template. Align the new Template 2 precisely on top of the woriginal Template 2 and trace hints from the original. Set Template 2 aside. Now add seam allowance to Template 1 and cut it out.

Here's a sneak peek at the finished center.
In real life, you would not sew
the units together at this point.

Example 1
Sometimes the links you investigate lead to a mirror image Patch 2.

Tiny dots clustered at the center help camouflage awkward or uneven seams.

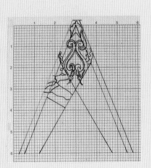

The master template

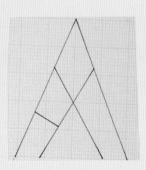

The diagram

Make separate templates for Patch 1 and Patch 2L.

Cut out the patches.

Patch 1 joined to Patch 2L and Patch 2R. In normal construction, you would complete the wedge design before joining Patch 2R to avoid the awkward Y seam.

The finished design.

Example 2

Keep in mind that the center of the kaleidoscope, where the tips of the wedges come together, is the most difficult position to sew. Don't expect all eight tips to connect dead-on. Instead of filling the top quarter inch with one highly contrasted, centered dot or a collection of mirror image curlicues, try exposing $\frac{1}{8}$″ to $\frac{1}{4}$″ of forgiving color. In the sewn-together center, color will meet color. A little more or a little less due to a slightly skewed seam won't really matter.

This example shows how I changed a complex center-in-progress to one that would be a little more forgiving when the wedges were ultimately joined.

The initial Patch 1/Patch 2 link

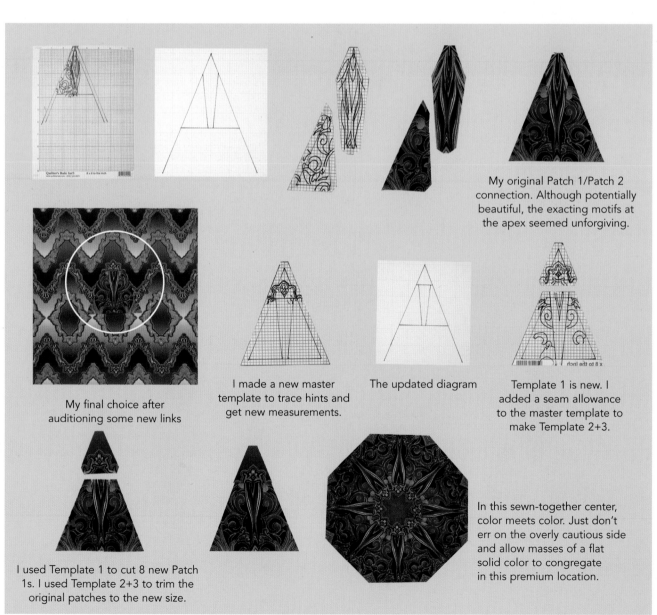

My original Patch 1/Patch 2 connection. Although potentially beautiful, the exacting motifs at the apex seemed unforgiving.

My final choice after auditioning some new links

I made a new master template to trace hints and get new measurements.

The updated diagram

Template 1 is new. I added a seam allowance to the master template to make Template 2+3.

I used Template 1 to cut 8 new Patch 1s. I used Template 2+3 to trim the original patches to the new size.

In this sewn-together center, color meets color. Just don't err on the overly cautious side and allow masses of a flat solid color to congregate in this premium location.

Finding the Link

Students always ask me, as I paw through their stash, what am I looking for? To paraphrase Jim Chee, a recurring fictional Navajo police officer in Tony Hillerman's mysteries, I'm not looking for anything in particular because then I might not see what I'm not looking for.

What I can tell you is that, instead of looking at a piece of fabric as a whole, I concentrate on the individual elements. Fabrics that look like they landed from different planets often unite in flawless connections, usually because an incidental doodad from one links unexpectedly with a partial motif in the other. It's hard to explain, but you'll know you've crossed over to an altered state of fabric consciousness when you find yourself concentrating on the details in a fabric's interior and ignoring the gestalt.

Paradoxically, this narrowed perspective widens the selection. The secondary components of a print take on an active life of their own. You will probably discover more relationships than you can use. Some connections crackle with drama, while others are so tranquil, it hardly seems worth the effort to sew the pieces together because the result looks like a continuation of the same fabric. But it's not the same fabric, and when multiplied eight times, those subtle changes in color and texture will emerge as elegant visual rhythms.

During this process, promise me you won't take it personally if a successful resolution takes longer than you anticipated. There isn't a right answer to the question "How long should it take?" Do you think it makes you more clever if you figure it out faster? When your design instincts point you in another direction, don't think of the original idea as a mistake. This puts a negative slant on a natural event in the creative process. Relish the ideas that propel you further along a path of creativity. Sometimes getting from a boring "here" to an inspired "there" takes lots of stops in between. Be grateful that your critical thinking skills kicked in, rather than bemoan the fact that they kicked in late. Personally, I'm a fast talker but a slow thinker. More often than not, it takes a lot of mulling time before I sense where my fabrics and I should go.

HOW TO CONTINUE THE DESIGN

There is no one single way to continue a piece in progress. Visual invention means never knowing what direction the design will take until you get there. At first, the potential for seemingly endless possibilities may be overwhelming. But experience has taught me that there is no absolute, correct, best selection and that fabric choices made today will be different from ones made tomorrow. Embracing the opportunities offered by choice rather than feeling challenged by them is liberating. Becoming a kaleidoscope aficionado has made me more adaptable and creative, both artistically and intellectually. After all, a breathtaking collision of color in a scope will maneuver into something different, something slightly new, during the very instant it takes me to hand it to you.

When you don't know what the next step is, it's probably time to make a template. If I'm pretty sure I'm looking for a fussy-cut rather than a stripped-on allover to fill this spot, the first step is to make a template for this space even before I search for potential fabrics. Then, when auditioning reveals the chosen motif, you can grab the already-made template, position it exactly on the motif and trace hints from the fabric onto the template, thereby securing your selection before it gets lost. To complete the transaction, count grid lines and transfer the patch's measurements from the template to the graph paper diagram.

To make a template for the next available space, I put template plastic over the area that needs to be filled and trace the available space, even if I think I might eventually break it up into two or more patches, rather than fill it up with one single fabric. In this case, I didn't have to line up bold lines from the template plastic to the bold lines of the graph paper because the patch doesn't fall on the center axis, although I do keep the orientation of the two grids identical, even if it means using more template plastic. Ignoring the grids' orientation will come back and haunt you, so keep them similar. Next, add seam allowance and directional cues. Since at this point I don't know how big Patch 3L will be, I cut it out bigger than it probably will end up and trim it to fit the chosen motif directly on the fabric. Don't be stingy; it's easy to trim, but if a template is too small for the final version, that means throwing away this one and making another. Don't forget to include enough template plastic for any additional $\frac{1}{4}$″ seam allowances.

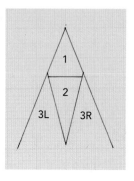

It's time to pose that hypothetical but strategic question favored by creative thinkers, scientists, philosophers, and artists alike: "What if?"

What if, I ask myself, looking for the answer as my mind's eye skims through unruly mounds of fabric heaped on the floor. Whatever catches my eye ends up in my hand. I can scan and discard ten fabrics in minutes. Other times, I'm more obsessive-compulsive. Something in the pile calls out that it deserves serious consideration, and I sit there and work it and work it, angling for a slightly different connection, making it unravel its hidden potential, just for me.

I audition links between Patch 2 and a potential Fabric 3 by physically placing the fabric against Patch 2's seamline. First, fold under $\frac{1}{4}$″ of Patch 2's seam allowance

so you're evaluating the true seamline in relationship to potential neighbors. Look for spots where the connection dissolves and appears seemingly seamless.

Or, what if you want to create a shape or line? Then look for contrast. If you don't know where to start, look at the fabric as a whole. Start where your eye is caught, perhaps by a warm glow or dramatic flash. Let the template take you into nooks and crannies that didn't seem interesting before. Move it a teensy bit to catch a shadowy beam; tweak it to include a curl. Then pick it up and try again.

HOW TO MARK THE DIAGRAM

It's usually easiest to take all measurements by starting from the apex of the triangle. Remember, when you initially drafted the angle, the apex was fixed at the intersection of two bold lines in order to use the graph paper as a ruler, so take advantage of the fact that you can jump from bold line to bold line and count inches and eighths of an inch quickly.

The pattern on one side of the center axis is the mirror image of the pattern on the other side. This insight means that I don't have to draw sewing lines over the entire triangle but on one side only. Flipping a template over to mark and cut patches, instead of creating a second template, ensures the lines stay fixed. I mark all my sewing lines on the left side of the diagram.

If a template is too complex to draft by counting gridlines, try this technique:

1. Place the template on the graph paper diagram in its proper position.

2. Align the edge of a ruler along the template's seamline— the one you are transferring to the diagram—allowing the ruler's ends to extend beyond the template and onto the graph paper.

3. Use a pencil to draw a light line along the edge of the ruler that is extending the seamline onto the graph paper diagram.

4. Remove the template, realign the ruler, and connect the pencil lines.

5. Erase any lines that fall outside the patch. This marking sequence accurately places the sewing line.

CONTINUOUS TEMPLATES

We've already talked about finding different backgrounds that visually blend and camouflage the seams. Another option is to fill adjacent patches with one and the same fabric in such a way the audience perceives that single fabric to be continuous from patch to patch. I used this effect in the background of *Kaleidoscopic XVI: More Is More*. Thirty-three kaleidoscopes dance on what appears to be a background uninterrupted by seams.

In this next example, I want the motif in Patch 1 to continue down the wedge's sides into Patch 2L and 2R. To pull this off, I've got to make the motif in Patch 2 resume at exactly the point where it ended in Patch 1.

Now that we understand the setup, we can formulate the question: how do you get that specific portion of motif to wend its way onto the template?

The key to this construction strategy is to align Templates 1 and 2 in an unusual way: after choosing the motif for Patch 1, position the two templates on the fabric by overlapping the seam allowance of Template 2 onto the seam allowance of Template 1, seamline on top of seamline.

Trace hints onto each template, taking care to copy lots of clues in both overlapping seam allowances (this means carefully removing each template in turn so you can trace hints on it while it's the layer closer to the fabric).

Also trace lots of hints along the seams where matching is most essential. I like to copy enough hints to make identifying repeats a cinch.

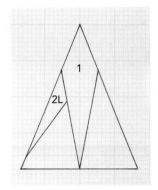  

The graph paper diagram | Make templates 1 and 2. | Align seamline on top of seamline.

Place the aligned templates on the fabric to see the seamless connection.

Mark plenty of clues.

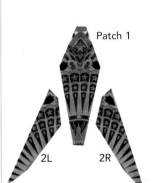

Patch 1

2L 2R

Cut and join the patches. | The assembled wedges

This template technique assures accurate patch alignment because it takes into account the all-important seam allowance—so you don't have to think about it. What have we learned from this? Templates made from see-through material are good.

Power Piecing

Prima donna patches must be cut and sewn one by one, but I've devised a shortcut, based on strip piecing, for adding odd-shaped, lilliputian-size allover fabrics. Because an allover pattern looks exactly the same from any angle, I don't need to worry about how the template falls. Long story short: sew a strip of allover fabric to its neighbor (it could be a fussy-cut patch, a pieced unit, or another allover), make one template incorporating both patches, and cut out both simultaneously. The result is a two-patch unit, complete with seam allowance, that looks like it was born that way.

Example 1

 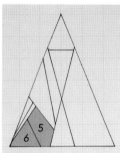

I want the intricate motif selected for Patch 5 to float on the background. To create this effect, I based my fabric choice for Patch 6 on the background color of the prima donna fabric used for Patch 5. (See Common Ground, page 72.)

1. Trace the motif for Patch 5 onto Template 5 and use it to cut out the appropriate number of patches.

2. Make a template that encompasses Patch 5 and Patch 6. Add a ¼″ seam allowance all around and cut out. Using a ruler, extend the seamline into the seam allowance at each end to ensure accurate placement along the full length of the sewing line. Align Template 5+6 on Template 5 and transfer the hints.

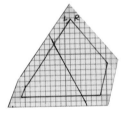 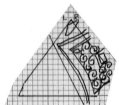

3. Rotary cut strips of Fabric 6. The strip(s) must be long enough to accommodate the number of patches needed altogether. (See Calculating Strip Width, page 112.)

4. Place Patch 5 on a Fabric 6 strip, right sides together, aligning the edges to be joined. Machine stitch. Repeat, sewing all the units at the same time, assembly line style. Remember that half the units must be reversed.

5. Press the seam allowance toward the darker patch. Position Template 5+6 on one stripped-together unit. Match the hints drawn on the template to the corresponding motifs in Patch 5+6. Align the sewing line marked on the template with the seam made in Step 4.

6. Hold the template firmly in place and trace around it to mark a visible, precise line on the Fabric 6 strip. Cut out Patch 5+6, using either a scissors or a small rotary cutter, aiming down the middle of the marked line.

7. Repeat Step 5 until you have enough accurately pieced units, each one complete with seam allowance and ready for its next assignment. Doesn't it look as if the patches were meticulously cut and pieced together?

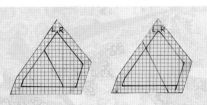

Once the seam allowance is added to a template, any marked lines representing seamlines are confined to the interior. It's much more useful if these lines travel from cut edge to cut edge. Take the time to extend all the sewing lines into the seam allowance to ensure accurate placement along the full length of the sewing line.

EXAMPLE 2

Here's a slightly different scenario. In this case, both Patch 5 and Patch 6 will be filled with allovers. Because there is no prima donna fabric involved, neither patch needs its own template.

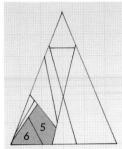

1. Make Template 5+6, add a ¼″ seam allowance, and cut out. Extend the seamline into the seam allowance.

2. Rotary cut strips of both fabrics.

3. Sew the two strips together. Press the seam allowance toward the wider patch.

4. Position Template 5+6 on top, aligning the sewing line marked on the template with the seam made in Step 3. Trace around the edge of the template. Repeat to mark the appropriate number of 5+6 L patches. Flip the template over to mark the same number of 5+6 R patches. Cut out.

Calculating Strip Width

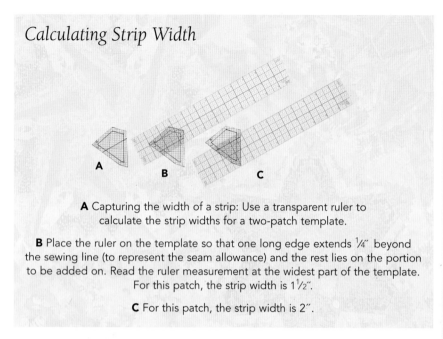

A Capturing the width of a strip: Use a transparent ruler to calculate the strip widths for a two-patch template.

B Place the ruler on the template so that one long edge extends ¼″ beyond the sewing line (to represent the seam allowance) and the rest lies on the portion to be added on. Read the ruler measurement at the widest part of the template. For this patch, the strip width is 1½″.

C For this patch, the strip width is 2″.

EXAMPLE 3

Fabrics with colors that merge together, blurring the seamline, can be good candidates for strip piecing.

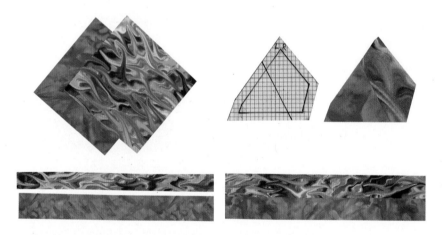

EXAMPLE 4

Here's a way to achieve a striped effect by strip piecing.

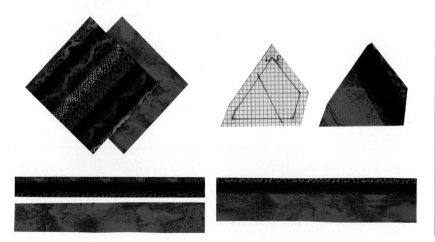

THE FINE POINTS & PERKS OF STRIP PIECING

The foremost benefit of strip piecing is obvious: you look like a piecing wizard. Not to mention you get to add diminutive, uncommonly shaped pieces without having to cut and stitch impossibly tiny patches. The rule is simple: never make a template for one lonesome allover. A patch comprising a single allover fabric does not need its own template.

There is no limit to the number of strips that can be added to a unit. Attach one at a time, one per template. For complex pieced units, like the intricate, branched extensions projecting from a snowflake, I sometimes draft a unit starting with two allovers stripped together in the middle, and then add two strips with each additional template, one strip to each side.

The second-best benefit is the opportunity to trim patches to the newest template. I try my best, but between sewing and pressing and handling, stuff stretches. Every new template made to guide a strip-piecing procedure is an opportunity to correct the piece-in-progress and pull it back in line with the graph paper diagram. Assume the newest, just-made template is accurate and align it to the prima donna. Next, position the template's sewing line directly on top of the actual seamline. If you have to fudge—and you will—let the allover, not the prima donna, make amends. Once the template is aligned, trim off any fabric sticking out beyond the template. I trim a lot, often using the handy-dandy Brooklyn Revolver, a circular rotary mat mounted on a lazy Susan.

Strip piecing also lends support to a patchwork assembled from mostly off-grain pieces. A stabilizing quality is added to the entire assemblage every time a strip cut along the grain is used.

Check out the wrong side of this patch.
See how the seam allowance extends beyond the necessary ¼"?
Use common sense and trim off the excess tidbits.
Strip-pieced units usually need to be pruned.

POWER PRESSING

Sewing narrow pieces means the ¼" seam allowance is sometimes bigger than some portion of its patch. Put a passel of puny patches side by side and the excess bulk starts bumping into the sewing machine's seam guide, causing it to bounce off its straight path. To prepare multiple layers for smoother stitching, press after every piecing sequence, toward the bigger patch if possible. Press into submission, making each seam lie as flat as possible.

Sometimes you're forced to press toward the smaller patch. For instance, if a bunch of seams already coexist in a tight area, it may be impossible to press the just-sewn strip in any direction except the way it naturally flops. In these cases, let the seam do its thing. Press as flat as you can using all your body weight.

HOW TO PIECE IRREGULAR SHAPES

Kaleidoscopic XVII: Caribbean Blues is divided into three large patched units by two long vertical seams. If the vertical seamlines were perfectly parallel, there'd be no trouble: the angles being sewn at the cut edges of the long seams would be identical. But because my lines aren't parallel, rather than assuming they are the same angle, I have to assume they are not. If you treat them without regard for this difference, as minute as it may seem in some examples, the resulting seam will be distorted.

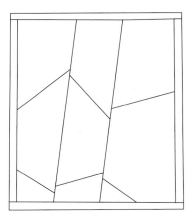

Quilt diagram, *Kaleidoscopic XVII: Caribbean Blues*

On the back of the patched unit, using the scant side of the 6″ C-Thru ruler, lightly mark—so it is not visible on the front—¼″ along the two edges that form corner A. Where the lines cross each other is the actual sewing point (Point A). This procedure always involves four corner points (A, B, C, D) because an accurate match extends from cut edge to cut edge. Repeat this procedure at each corner. Pin right sides together, matching sewing point to sewing point (A to C, B to D), to position the fabric shapes together accurately.

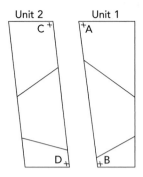

I use this procedure any time I have to sew irregularly shaped units together and, for some reason, their corners haven't been trimmed as described in Matching Templates, page 97.

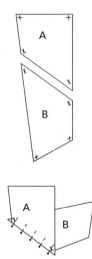

MASTER TEMPLATES

With Seam Allowance

The best way to repair a flawed piece-of-pie is with a Master Template. Line up a sheet of template plastic to the graph paper diagram, matching the center axis of the diagram to a bold inch line on the template plastic grid. Trace the 45° angle onto the template plastic. Copy a few of the longest or most vital sewing

lines. Trace enough lines from the original to provide cues for aligning the Master Template to the piece of patchwork pie. Add seam allowance. A big wedge may require two sheets of template plastic taped together (make sure you align the grids). Or, make a template of one half of the triangle and flip it over to investigate the other side.

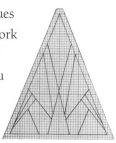

Master template with seam allowance

To use a Master Template, place it on the pieced wedge and align the all-important on-grain Patch 1 and the center axis. Don't expect every line on the template line to match a sewing line on the wedge of fabrics. Now, assess how and where the pieced triangle is off. Sometimes the seam allowance along the side seam is too narrow or too big. Sometimes identifying one unruly seam as the culprit is enough to adjust the design. Sometimes the mature, sensible thing to do is take a deep breath, rip, and repair.

A triangle that ends up too big can't be automatically fixed by chopping off the excess at the side seams. If the guilty party is an allover fabric, whack away, fitting the shape to the Master Template. A little more/a little less won't make much of a difference. But never trim a fussy cut that's primed to meet its identical twin without weighing the consequences. If only one is trimmed, the joint between two mirror image motifs is no longer the same. It's okay if one of twelve connections doesn't match. But if a pack of prima donnas is threatening to ruin the production, try a Master Template without seam allowance.

Without Seam Allowance

Another remedy for healing a warped wedge is to actually mark the sewing lines for the side seams on the wrong side of the finished triangle. Otherwise, there is an assumption that the edge of the completed fabric triangle is accurate and can be used to align to the neighboring triangle. For this cure, you'll need to make a full-size Master Template without seam allowance.

Master template without seam allowance

Align the Master Template to the wrong side of the fabric triangle, first to Patch 1, then to the center axis, then along a couple of the long seams. Hold the template firmly in place and trace around the edge with a well-sharpened lead or chalk pencil or a somewhat dried-out permanent marker. The idea is to make a visible but pale line that doesn't bleed through to the front of the fabric. Next, join together by aligning the marked triangle with another wedge, right sides together, pinning together where the marked sewing line coincides at a seam joint. Sometimes marking both triangles is helpful even if only one is inaccurate. If the resulting seam allowance is very narrow—less than 1/4″—use a small stitch length and go over it a few times to reinforce the join.

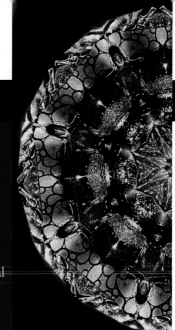

FINISHING

JOINING TOGETHER

This is the moment we've been waiting for. The whole becomes greater than the sum of its parts. Keep in mind that success is not about matching every single joint along all sixteen borders. A few mismatched points are simply not going to be noticed in a patchwork filled to the brim with complexity. The objective is to identify which junctions will be the most disruptive if they are slightly off. Season the usual rules of piecing with a generous dose of common sense. Remember, visual coherence is already guaranteed by the symmetry of identical sections radiating from a central point.

My policy is to focus on the prima donnas and fudge with the allovers. Examine the finished triangle along the seamline and locate areas of maximum value contrast. For example, a white line sitting against an indigo background makes for a strong contrast. Since the eye zooms in on areas of sharp contrasts, align these junctions carefully. The coupling between areas of soft contrast can be mildly awry, even downright wonky, without dissolving the illusion of seamless continuity from one wedge to the next.

Place two wedges right sides together, matching the corresponding patches and seamlines, and pin. I pin a lot, using thin, sharp pins. I rarely baste. It doesn't seem to make the alignment more accurate, especially when there's a double dose of bulky seams along the presser foot's intended route.

Begin by matching and pinning Patch 1 at the apex of the triangle to its twin in the second triangle. Next, align the prima donnas and areas of strong value contrast. Finally, ease in the more forgiving allovers. Here's where we benefit from the natural give of fabrics cut on the bias. Gently, but with forceful assurance, aim for neatly joined seams.

Sew the pair of triangles with a larger stitch and don't start and end with a knot. If any motifs wind up violently mismatched, a knot-free line of bigger stitches is easier to rip out. If the match is up to your standards, stitch over the seam. Sew slowly, using one setting smaller than the machine's default stitches-per-inch setting. Begin from the skinny tops of Patch 1 and sew toward the bottom, back-stitching at the beginning and end. If the presser foot bumps off the $1/4''$ seam, stop. Rip. Remove any leftover threads. Realign. Repin. Restitch, overlapping a few of the leftover previous stitches with new ones.

Press after every sequence. Press the long seams open if possible otherwise, press the inevitable thickness as flat as possible and ignore unavoidable imperfections. Even in a real kaleidoscope, every multifaceted image isn't reflected flawlessly. It depends on the optical quality of the mirrors, the critical angle of the mirror setup, and the seams where the mirrors connect. Just like its quilted counterpart, the scope maker's objective is to eliminate as many distractions as possible.

Octagon—45° Angle

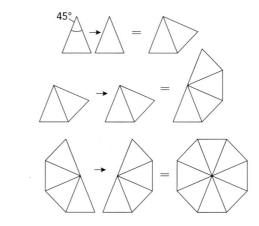

Piecing sequence for an eight-sided design

1. Sew each triangle to another, creating four pairs.

2. Piece one pair of triangles to another duo. Repeat, creating two sets of four.

3. Stop and look at these two four-triangle units. If an octagon equals 360°, then four wedges joined together equal half of that, or 180°. You might remember from high school geometry that a straight line equals 180°, and if you don't, I'm telling you right now. Therefore, four patches sewn together must form a straight line. If your triangles look like this

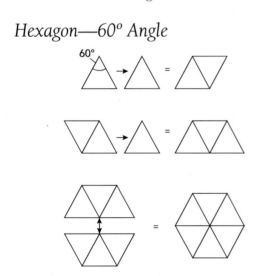

or this,

don't expect them to join together in 360° harmony. Analyze and make corrections using a Master Template, if necessary, before continuing the piecing sequence. The error is probably due to an inaccurate seam between two wedges.

4. Sew the two halves together.

Hexagon—60° Angle

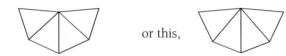

Piecing sequence for a six-sided design

1. Sew one triangle to another. Repeat one time only, creating two pairs.

2. Stitch one triangle to each of the pairs, creating two units comprised of three triangles each.

3. Follow Octagon Step 3 to make any needed adjustments.

4. Sew the two halves together.

Decagon—36° Angle

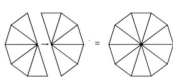

Piecing sequence for a ten-sided design

A ten-sided design is quirky. Divide 360° into ten pieces of the pie and you get a slim 36° wedge. When all ten converge at a single point, expect a densely packed crowd.

1. Sew four triangles to four other triangles, making four pairs.

2. Piece one pair of triangles to another pair. Repeat, creating two units of four triangles.

3. Add one triangle to each of the units, creating two halves of five triangles.

4. Follow Octagon Step 3 to make any needed adjustments.

5. Sew the two halves together.

SQUARING OFF

Adding a right triangle to four of the eight or six wedges turns an octagon into a square and a hexagon into a rectangle, ready to frame or combine into a quilt. A ten-sided design requires dredging up geometry from some previous life.

Octagon

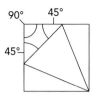
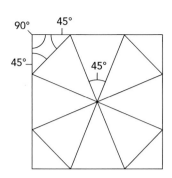

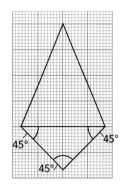

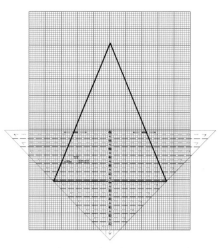

Adding a right triangle to
the piece-of-pie

Using a right triangle ruler to create the corner
triangle for an eight-sided kaleidoscope

The easiest way to calculate the right-angled triangle for a specific sized wedge is to draft the triangle to the bottom of the original graph paper diagram; be sure to include room for this addition. Place a triangle or square rotary ruler so the center line is aligned with the center axis. Orient the long side of the ruler by lining it to the very last line of the piece-of-pie. Slowly slide the ruler toward the top of the graph paper triangle. Stop when the edges of the ruler touch the corners of the piece-of-pie exactly. This is the size and shape of the required corner patch. Holding the ruler securely in place, use its straight edges to trace this shape on the graph paper. Make a template, adding seam allowance to every side of the template.

Hexagon

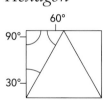
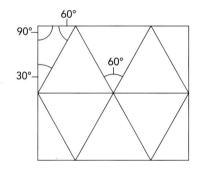
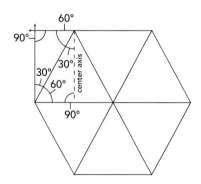

Calculating the dimensions of this 30°-60°-90° corner triangle requires no gadgetry. It simply equals one half of the piece-of-pie. The vertical of the long corner triangle is the same length as the center axis. Make a plastic template of the corner triangle, adding ¼" seam allowance to each edge. You will need to cut four corner triangles—two L's and two R's (reverse the template)—to complete your hexagon block.

Decagon

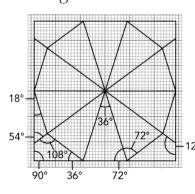

The corners of a ten-sided design require finesse because a single, right-angled triangle is not the solution.

A 10-sided design
with 36° triangles

WORKBOOK

KALEIDOSCOPE A

1

2

3

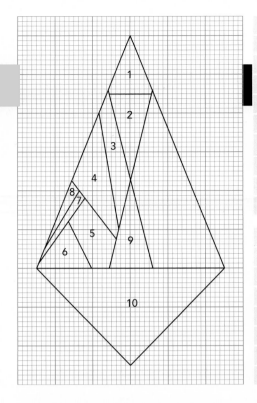

Template 1	Cut 8.
Template 2	Cut 8.
Template 3	Cut 8L and 8R.
Template 4	Cut 8L and 8R.
Template 5	Cut 8L and 8R.
Template 5+6	Strip Fabric 6 to Patch 5. Cut 8L and 8R.
Template 5+6+7	Strip Fabric 7 to Patch (5+6). Cut 8L and 8R.
Template 5+6+7+8	Strip Fabric 8 to Patch (5+6+7). Cut 8L and 8R.
Template 9	Cut 8.
Template 10	Cut 4.

Sew Patch 1, 2, 3L and 4L together.	8x
Sew Patch (5+6+7+8)L to Patch (1+2)+(3+4)L.	8x
Sew Patch 3R to Patch 4R.	8x
Sew Patch (5+6+7+8)R to Patch (3+4)R.	8x
Sew Patch 9 to Patch (3+4+5+6+7+8)R.	8x
Sew Patch (1+2)+(3+4+5+6+7+8)L to Patch 9 + (3+4+5+6+7+8)R.	8x
Sew 8 wedges together.	1x
Add Patch 10.	4x

4

5

6 and 10

7

8

9

1

2

3

4

5

6

7

8

9

These swatches were auditioned for Patch 8.

Template 1	Cut 8.
Template 2	Cut 8.
Template 3	Cut 8.
Template 4	Cut 8L and 8R.
Template 5	Cut 8L and 8R.
Template 6	Cut 8L and 8R.
Template 7	Cut 8L and 8R.
Template 4+5+6+7+8	Strip Fabric 8 to Patch (4+5+6+7). Cut 8L and 8R.
Template 9	Cut 4.

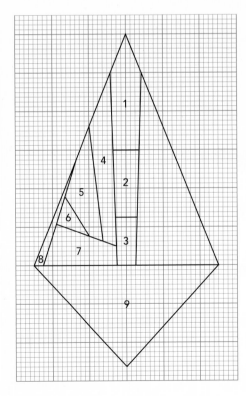

Sew Patch 1, 2, and 3 together.	8x
Sew Patch 4L to Patch 5L and Patch 4R to 5R.	8x
Sew Patch 6L to (4+5)L and Patch 6R to (4+5)R.	8x
Sew Patch 7L to (4+5+6+7)L and Patch 7R to (4+5+6+7)R.	8x
Sew Patch (4+5+6+7+8)L to Patch (1+2+3).	8x
Sew Patch (4+5+6+7+8)R to Patch (1+2+3)+(4+5+6+7+8)L.	8x
Sew 8 wedges together.	1x
Add Patch 9.	4x

KALEIDOSCOPE QUILT TRIANGLE MEASUREMENTS

5 Slices – 72° each		6 Slices – 60° each		8 Slices – 45° each		10 Slices – 36° each		12 Slices – 30° each		16 Slices – 22.5° each	
Vertical	Horizontal	Vertical	Horizontal	Vertical	Horizontal	Vertical	Horizontal	Vertical	Horizontal	Vertical	Horizontal
1⅜"	1"	2⅜"	1⅜"	1½"	⅝"	4⅝"	1½"	1⅞"	½"	1¼"	¼"
2¾"	2"	3¼"	1⅞"	3⅝"	1½"	9⅝"	3⅛"	3¼"	⅞"	2½"	½"
4⅛"	3"	5⅝"	3¼"	5⅛"	2⅛"	10"	3¼"	5⅛"	1⅜"	6½"	1¼"
5½"	4"	6½"	3¾"	7¼"	3"	14⅝"	4¾"	7"	1⅞"	10⅜"	2"
10½"	7⅝"	8⅞"	5⅛"	8¾"	3⅝"	15"	4⅞"	8⅞"	2⅜"	15"	2⅞"
11⅞"	8⅝"	12⅛"	7"	12⅜"	5⅛"	20"	6½"	12⅛"	3¼"	20⅛"	4"
13¼"	9⅝"	14½"	8⅜"	16"	6⅝"	24⅝"	8"	14"	3¾"	20¾"	4⅛"
14⅝"	10⅝"	15⅜"	8⅞"	17½"	7¼"	25"	8⅛"	19⅛"	5⅛"	22"	4⅜"
16"	11⅝"	17¾"	10¼"	21⅛"	8¾"			21"	5⅝"	22⅝"	4½"
17⅜"	12⅝"	21"	12⅛"	24¾"	10¼"			24¼"	6½"	23⅞"	4¾"
18¾"	13⅝"	24¼"	14"							24½"	4⅞"
20⅛"	14⅝"										

Vertical = length along center axis

Horizontal = left and right distance from center axis

Formulated by Sue Helzer, College Park, MD

ABOUT THE AUTHOR

Paula Nadelstern combines the symmetry and surprise of a kaleidoscope with the techniques and materials of quiltmaking. The color and complexity of Paula's quilts invite the reader to return again and again.

In addition to her numerous awards, Paula has received Artist's Fellowships from the New York Foundation for the Arts and the Bronx Council on the Arts. Her work has also been showcased in publications and exhibits worldwide. Paula designs textile prints exclusively for Benartex. She lives in New York City with her husband, Eric.

Photo by Marianne Barcellona

ACKNOWLEDGMENTS

Until I met quilts, I thought I was creative but not talented. To find something you love to do is a gift. To achieve recognition for it is a miracle. The following people and companies deserve my gratitude for supporting me as I found my way. I especially want to acknowledge the role of my editor, Candie Frankel, who always manages to prop me up in her competent, comforting way—I wouldn't have wanted to do this without her. Also, extreme kudos goes to my Team C&T: Helen Frost, Kristen "Not-Afraid-of-Color" Yenche, and Kesel Wilson. They worked and listened very hard to make me look good.

Amy Marson, Todd Hensley, Luke Mulks, Diane Pedersen, Zinnia Heinzmann, Jan Grigsby, Lynn Koolish, John Pilcher (C&T Publications) • Stacy Hollander (The American Folk Art Museum) • Karen Bell • George Gottlieb, Marc Misthal • Clara Lyman • Eva Nadelstern • Amy Orr • Robin Schwalb • Katherine Knauer • Shirley Levine • Jeanne Butler • Wendy Richardson (Quilt Tapestry Studios) • Deb Tilley • Linda Joy • Shelley Knapp • Michael Miron • Stevii Graves • Lorraine Torrence • Ludmila Aristova • Teresa Barkley • Randy Frost •Iris Gowen • Tatiana Ivina •Emiko Toda Loeb • Ruth Marchese • Jeri Riggs • Diana Robinson • Sandra Sider • Arle Sklar-Weinstein • Daphne Taylor • Ludmila Uspenskaya • Erin Wilson •Adrienne Yorinks • Megan Downer, Katia Hoffman, David Lochner, Karlos DeSalla, Susan Neill, Susan Kemler Tazzi, Alex Rodriguez, Bill Mason, Gayle Camargo (Benartex Fabrics) • Martin Favre, Gayle Hillert, Jeanne C. Delpit (Bernina of America) • Pat Yamin (Come Quilt With Me) • H.D. Wilbanks, Darlene Christopherson (Hobbs Bonded Fabrics) • Marti Michell (Michell Marketing) • Peggy Schaefer (Omnigrid, a division of Prym/Dritz) • Ted Finkelstein, Miranda Stewart (Gutermann of America, Inc.) • Rowenta Irons • Cheryl Little (The Cotton Club) • Linda Crouch, Linda Kaiser, Brenda Crouch (Tennessee Quilts) • Lucy Mansfield (The Quilt Scene) • Evie Ashworth (Robert Kaufman Fabrics) • Ricky Tims, Anna Fishman (Red Rooster Fabrics) • Lonni Rossi, Clifford Quibell, Gail Kessler (Andover Fabrics) • Donna Wilder, Meredith Voltaggio, Debi Porreca (FreeSpirit) • Sandy Muckenthaler (Hoffman Fabrics) • Jason and Sharon Yenter (In the Beginning Fabrics) • Shelley and Randy Knapp • Charles Karadimos • Carol and Tom Paretti • Steve and Peggy Kittelson • Paul and Susan Knox • Al Teich • David Sugich • Sue Rioux • Bob Rioux •

SOURCES

For a list of other fine books from C&T Publishing, ask for a free catalog:

C&T PUBLISHING, INC.

P.O. Box 1456

Lafayette, CA 94549

(800) 284-1114

Email: ctinfo@ctpub.com

Website: www.ctpub.com

C&T Publishing's professional photography services are now available to the public. Visit us at www.ctmediaservices.com.

For quilting supplies:

COTTON PATCH

1025 Brown Ave.

Lafayette, CA 94549

(800) 835-4418 or

(925) 283-7883

Email: CottonPa@aol.com

Website: www.quiltusa.com

Note: Fabrics used in the quilts shown may not be currently available, as fabric manufacturers keep most fabrics in print for only a short time.

GUIDE TO NYC GARMENT DISTRICT

Website: www.paulanadelstern.com

BENARTEX

1359 Broadway, #1100, Dept PN

New York, NY 10036

Website: www.benartex.com

Inquire about fabric collections designed by Paula Nadelstern.

THE COTTON CLUB

P.O. Box 2263

Boise, ID 83701

(208) 345-5567

Email: cotton@cottonclub.com

Website: www.cottonclub.com

Source for Paula's fabric collections, prints with symmetrical motifs, see-through gridded template plastic, rulers, and eight-squares-to-the-inch graph paper pads.

COME QUILT WITH ME

3903 Avenue I

Brooklyn, NY 11210

Phone or fax: (718) 377-3652

Source for the Brooklyn Revolver, a circular rotary cutting mat on a lazy Susan.

DICK BLICK

(800) 447-8192

Website: www.dickblick.com

Comprehensive art supply catalog; source for pens and graph paper pads.

DISPLAYAWAY

(888) ITS SAFE [487-7233]

Email: Zellerwood@aol.com

Clever, safe, attractive display system allows quilts to be hung and removed in minutes.

INTERNATIONAL FABRIC COLLECTION

3445 West Lake Road

Erie, PA 16505-3661

(800) 462-3891

Liberty of London Tana Lawn; fusible interfacing.

QUILTER'S RULE INTERNATIONAL, LLC

817 Mohr Avenue

Waterford, WI 53185

(800) 343-8671

Website: www.quiltersrule.com

TGR-8: clear see-through template plastic printed with turquoise $1/8''$ grid and bold one-inch lines. Packages of four $8 1/2'' \times 11''$ sheets

QUILTINGPRO

Email: Tgavin@quiltingpro.com

Management software for cataloging quilts and tracking shows and expenses.

STEINLAUF & STOLLER

239 West 39th Street

New York, NY 10018

(212) 869-0321

(877) 869-0321 (toll-free)

Website: www.steinlaufandstoller.com

Notions distributor and source for featherweight fusible interfacing (CL FW); $30.00 minimum.

Index

A

allovers, 85–87

  amount to buy, 87

  as background, 72

  compared to prima donnas, 85

  dots and dashes, 86

  prints, 86

  reads like a solid, 85

American Meteorological Society, 30

axis of reflection, 73, 92

axis of symmetry, 73

B

background

  black, 19, 56

  complex and animated, 35

  as part of wedge, 16–17, 24

  receding, 31, 56, 71, 72–73

  for snowflakes, 31

  textured, 60

batik, 87

  African, 38

  dye process, 27, 87

  mirror image motifs, 27, 87

beading, 44

Bell, Karen, 73

Bentley, W. A., 30

bilateral symmetrical fabric, 80–81, 101

border

  creation of, 57

  fabric for, 60

bowing, 100

  cause of, 100

  compensating for, 100

Brewster, David, Sir, 33

Brooklyn Bridge, 59, 60

Brooklyn Revolver, 113

butterfly effect, 73, 80, 92, 101

C

camouflaging seams, 24, 27, 35, 70–71, 86

as an invitation to view more closely, 35

  with prints, 86

central axis, 73

chai, 19

chaos theory, 74–75

Chee, Jim, 107

"chorus line," 41

classic stripes, 83

clues, 97, 103, 109

common ground, 72–73

compass, 8, 77, 90

concentric circles, 8–9, 47

continuous templates, 49, 109

couching, 44, 59, 61

C-Thru ruler, 77, 90, 95

  how to use, 95, 103, 108, 111, 113

curves, illusory, 13, 64, 77–78

cutting patches off-grain, 77

cutting tools, 90, 101

D

decagon, 21, 116, 117

DELTA II limited edition kaleidoscope, 19

design and sewing sequence, 68–69

design-technique interface, 68

design wall, 90

dichroic glass, 12

dog-ears, how to trim, 98, 113

F

fabric

  auditioning, 64, 70–71, 72, 73, 75, 76, 79–87, 81, 83, 94, 101–107, 110, 121

  avoiding true solids, 85

  cutting, 101

  direction of pattern in, 79, 85

  does not need to match, 78, 79

  estimating yardage, 87

  marking, 100

  with mirror image motifs, 82

for Patch 1, 81

  selection, 118–121

  shopping for, 25, 52

  for strip piecing, 85

fabric grain, 77, 101, 113

fabric palette

  descriptors for, 31, 64

fabric types, 80–87

  allovers, 85–86

  bilateral symmetrical, 80–81

  classic stripes, 83

  dots and dashes, 86

  ombré, 84

  prima donnas, 80–84

  prints, 86

  pseudosymmetrical, 73, 82, 109, 113, 121

  symbiotic, 84

  wacky stripes, 83

faux curves, 64, 77–78

Feldman, Susan, 93

figure-ground relationship, 74

focal point, absence of, 64

four-mirror system, 38–39, 41

fusible interfacing, to stabilize silk, 19, 25, 47, 87

fussy cuts. See prima donnas.

G

gel ink pen, 90, 100

George R. Brown Convention Center, 9

graph paper, 90, 92–93

  as design tool, 68

  how to use, 13, 68, 92–93, 103, 117

graph paper diagram, 109. See also wedge diagram

H

hand appliqué, 46, 47, 59, 61

Helzer, Sue, 93

hexagon, 116, 117

Hillerman, Tony, 107

Hilton Americas-Houston hotel, 9

how to

  add seam allowance to a template, 95

  add visual movement, 75, 76

  audition fabrics, 68, 70–71, 72, 76, 81, 83, 94, 101, 102–107, 108, 118–121

  avoid bulky seams, 69, 113

  calculate strip width, 112

  continue a fabric design, 107–109

  correct a flawed wedge, 114

  create a sense of depth, 75

  cut fabric, 101

  cut out a template, 95

  design a wedge, 118–121

  design seamless connections, 71

  draft an angle, 91–93

  draft the wedge diagram, 77, 78

  estimate fabric yardage, 87

  identify a symmetrical motif, 73

  investigate a link, 102–103, 105

  join irregular shapes, 113–114

  join wedges, 115–116

  make a Master Template, 114

  make a template, 94–95, 103–104

  make Templates 1 and 2, 103–106

  make templates match, 97–100

  mark a template, 95, 96, 97, 103

  mark fabric, 100

  mark the diagram, 103, 108

  press seams, 113

  "pulsate" a design, 74–75

  relate Patch 1 to Patch 2, 102–107

  simulate a curve, 77–78

  square off, 116–117

  strip piece, 110–113

use a compass, 77

use a C-Thru ruler, 77, 95, 103, 108, 111, 113

use graph paper, 68, 92–93, 103

use template plastic, 68, 102–103, 104, 108, 109, 114

view a quilt, 71

I

insets, avoiding, 69

Itchiku Kubota, 24

Itchiku Kubota Kimono Museum, 89

J

Japan, author's visit to, 49, 52, 89

K

kaleidoscope, 19, 33, 67, 74, 75, 76, 78

  defined, 67

  45°-45°-90° configuration, 33

  four-mirror system, 38–39, 41

  interior, 12, 76

  invention of, 33

  three-mirror system, 33

  two-mirror system, 33

Kaleidoscope A, 118–119

Kaleidoscope B, 76, 120–121

kaleidoscopic designs, characteristics of, 67

kaleidoscopic hotel carpet, 9

Karadimos, Charles, 19, 75

karesansui, 49

Kathy's Quilt limited edition kaleidoscope, 33

kimono "Gaudi," 24

kimono silk, 27, 52, 57, 60

  ombré, 57, 60

  width of, 52, 57

Knapp Studio, 76, 94

Kubota-san, 89

L

lazy Susan, 113

lighting, 90

linear layout, 56

line of symmetry, 92